Timed Readings

FIFTY 400-WORD PASSAGES
WITH QUESTIONS FOR
BUILDING READING SPEED

Book Two

EDWARD SPARGO
GLENN R. WILLISTON
LINDA BROWNING

 JAMESTOWN PUBLISHERS
PROVIDENCE, RHODE ISLAND

TIMED READINGS
No. 802, Book 2

Copyright © 1980 by Jamestown Publishers, Inc.

Cover Design by Stephen R. Anthony

Illustrations by Mari-Ann Süvari

Printed in the United States
79 80 81 82 9 8 7 6 5 4 3

ISBN 0-89061-199-8

Contents

To the Instructor

Timed Readings is designed to provide plentiful practice in building reading speed—and comprehension—using graded selections of standard word length.

The Reading Selections

For any drill to be productive and meaningful, all the elements of the practice, except the one being taught, should be held constant. In *Timed Readings* the selections in all ten books are 400 words long and all deal with factual information.

The variable element in the series is the reading level of the selections. Starting at grade four, each book advances one grade level, ending at college level. Readability of the selections was assessed by applying Fry's *Formula for Assessing Readability*, using two samples from each selection.

Placement in the Series

To become faster and better readers using *Timed Readings*, students must start at a suitable reading level. For speed practice this means one or two levels below the student's instructional level. For most average readers, a suitable level would probably be a reading level one or two grades below their present grade in school.

How Fast Is Fast?

What is the optimum rate for each reader? Only individual students can determine the limits to which they can be challenged. Just as timing elicits exceptional performance from the athlete, the irrepressible impulse of the reader to beat the clock can produce spectacular progress.

For many students a rate of 400 words a minute would be impressive, if sustained, on factual material of the type included in *Timed Readings*. However, this rate should not be imposed as a standard for everyone, nor should it be allowed to become a ceiling for talented students.

Timing the Selections

To help students time the selections, this method is suggested. Write on the blackboard these times:

:10	:20	:30	:40	:50	1:00
1:10	1:20	1:30	1:40	1:50	2:00
2:10	2:20	2:30	2:40	2:50	3:00
3:10	3:20	3:30	3:40	3:50	4:00
4:10	4:20	4:30	4:40	4:50	5:00

Give students the signal to preview. Allow 30 seconds for this.

Direct students to read the selection and begin timing. At the end of ten seconds, erase *:10;* ten seconds later, erase *:20;* ten seconds later, erase *:30,* and so on until all the numbers have been erased or all the students have finished reading.

Instruct students to look up to the board when they finish reading and copy the lowest time remaining—the next number to be erased. This is their reading time. This number should be written on the top line *(Reading Time)* in the timing box at the top of the page they have just read.

Scheduling the Pacing Drills

A feature of the revised edition of *Timed Readings* is the opportunity to offer pacing drills. Page 9 describes these drills and the value of them. A section addressed to the instructor discusses how and when the drills may be scheduled and how to set the pace for the drills.

The Comprehension Questions

No achiever can claim success until he or she has been tested. In the case of *Timed Readings,* speed without comprehension is meaningless. Students must display adequate comprehension before their rate can be considered valid. Comprehension scores of 70 to 80 percent indicate that learners are properly placed within the series and are comprehending satisfactorily.

The questions accompanying the selections were constructed with a single purpose in mind—to demonstrate that the reader has, in fact, read the selection. In this regard, the questions may be considered comprehension checks rather than comprehension tests. A mix of question types—five fact and five thought questions—accompanies each selection.

An answer key on pages 116 and 117 permits immediate correction of responses and reinforcement of learning.

The Progress Graph

Industry has discovered the usefulness of charts and graphs for employee motivation. The graphs on pages 118 and 119 help students visualize their progress and reinforce their incentive to progress even further. Encourage students to maintain comprehension scores of 70 to 80 percent while gradually increasing their reading rate.

The legend on the right-hand side of the progress graphs automatically converts reading times into words-per-minute reading rates.

Another graph is provided on page 120 for students to use to plot their success with the pacing drills.

Advancement to Successive Levels

A student who has reached a peak of reading speed (with satisfactory comprehension) is ready to advance to the next book in the *Timed Readings* series. For example, a student who consistently achieves a reading rate of 400 words per minute with 80 percent or higher comprehension might better be challenged to transfer this achievement to a higher and more difficult level in the series. However, students should be encouraged to maintain their rate on a number of selections in order to consolidate their achievement before moving on to the higher level.

How to Use This Book

1. Learn the Four Steps. Study and learn the four steps to follow to become a better and faster reader. The steps are covered on pages 10, 11, 12 and 13.

2. Find Reading Selection. Turn to the selection you are going to read and wait for the instructor's signal to preview. Your instructor will allow 30 seconds for previewing.

3. Begin Reading. When your instructor gives you the signal, begin reading. Read at a slightly faster-than-normal speed. Read well enough so that you will be able to answer questions about what you have read.

4. Fill in Timing Box. When you finish reading, look at the blackboard and note your reading time. Your reading time will be the lowest time remaining on the board, or the next number to be erased. Write this time in the timing box at the top of the page on the first line, *Reading Time*.

5. Answer Questions. Turn the page and answer the ten questions on the back. There are five fact questions and five thought questions. Pick the *best* answer to each question and put an *x* in that box.

6. Correct Your Answers. Using the Answer Key on pages 116 and 117, correct your work. Circle your wrong answers and put an *x* in the box you should have marked. Score 10 points for each correct answer. Write your score in the timing box on the second line, *Comprehension Score*.

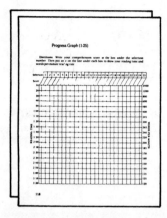

7. Fill in Progress Graph. Enter your score and plot your reading time on the graph on page 118 or 119. The right-hand side of the graph shows your words-per-minute reading speed. Write this number in the timing box on the bottom line, *Words per Minute.*

Instructions for the Pacing Drills

From time to time your instructor may wish to conduct pacing drills using *Timed Readings.* For this work you need to use the Pacing Dots printed in the margins of your book pages. These dots will help you regulate your reading speed to match the pace set by your instructor or announced on the cassette tape.

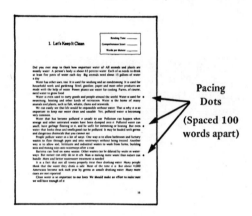

Pacing
Dots

(Spaced 100 words apart)

You will be reading at the correct pace if you are at the dot when your instructor says "Mark" or when you hear the tone on the tape. If you are ahead of the pace, read a little more slowly; if you are behind the pace, increase your reading speed. Try to match the pace exactly.

Follow these steps.

Step 1: Record the Pace. In the timing box at the top of the page, write on the line labeled *Words per Minute* the rate announced by the instructor or by the speaker on the tape.

Step 2: Begin Reading. Wait for the signal to begin reading. Read at a slightly faster-than-normal speed. You will not know how on-target your pace is until you hear your instructor say "Mark" or you hear the first tone on the tape. After a little practice you will be able to select an appropriate starting speed most of the time.

Step 3: Adjust Your Pace. As you read, try to match the pace set by the instructor or the tape. Read more slowly or more quickly as necessary. You should be reading the line beside a dot when you hear the pacing signal. The pacing sounds may distract you at first. Don't worry about it. Keep reading and your concentration will return.

Step 4: Stop and Answer Questions. Stop reading when you are told to, even if you have not finished the selection. Answer the questions right away. Correct your work and record your score in the timing box on the second line, *Comprehension Score.* Strive to maintain 80 percent comprehension on each drill as you gradually increase your pace.

Step 5: Fill in the Pacing Graph. Transfer your words-per-minute rate to the box labeled *Pace* on the pacing graph on page 120. Then plot your comprehension score on the line beneath the box.

These pacing drills are designed to help you become a more flexible reader. They encourage you to "break out" of a pattern of reading everything at the same speed.

The drills help in other ways, too. Sometimes in a reading program you reach a certain level and bog down. You don't seem able to move on and progress. These pacing drills will help you to work your way out of such slumps and get your reading program moving again.

To the Instructor

As a variation in the *Timed Readings* routine, try to schedule pacing drills at least once a week. Select an appropriate starting pace, one that is comfortable for everyone in the class. Do four or five drills, increasing the pace each time.

A Pacing Cassette is available which directs students through the drills. If you are not using the cassette, follow the guide at right to set the pace.

To set a pace of	
100 wpm, say "Mark" every	60 seconds
125	48
150	40
175	34
200	30
225	26
250	24
275	22
300	20
325	18
350	17
375	16
400	15
425	14
450	13
500	12
550	11
600	10
650	9
750	8
850	7
1000	6

Steps to Faster Reading

Step 1: Preview *When you read, do you start in with the first word, or do you look over the whole selection for a moment? Good readers preview the selection first— this helps to make them good, and fast, readers.*

1. Read the Title   The first thing to do when previewing is to read the title of the selection. Titles are designed not only to announce the subject, but also to make the reader think. What can you learn from the title? What thoughts does it bring to mind? What do you already know about this subject?

2. Read the Opening Paragraph   If the first paragraph is long, read the first sentence or two instead. The first paragraph is the writer's opportunity to greet the reader. He may have something to tell you about what is to come. Some writers announce what they hope to tell you in the selection. Some writers tell why they are writing. Some writers just try to get the reader's attention—they may ask a provocative question.

3. Read the Closing Paragraph   If the last paragraph is long, read just the final line or two. The closing paragraph is the writer's last chance to talk to his reader. He may have something important to say at the end. Some writers repeat the main idea once more. Some writers draw a conclusion: this is what they have been leading up to. Some writers summarize their thoughts; they tie all the facts together.

4. Glance through   Scan the selection quickly to see what else you can pick up. Discover whatever you can to help you read the selection. Are there names, dates, numbers? If so, you may have to read more slowly. Are there colorful adjectives? The selection might be light and fairly easy to read. Is the selection informative, containing a lot of facts, or conversational, an informal discussion with the reader?

Steps to Faster Reading

Step 2: Read for Meaning

When you read, do you just see words? Are you so occupied reading words that you sometimes fail to get the meaning? Good readers see beyond the words—they read for meaning. This makes them faster readers.

1. Build Concentration

You cannot read with understanding if you are not concentrating. Every reader's mind wanders occasionally; it is not a cause for alarm. When you discover that your thoughts have strayed, correct the situation right away. The longer you wait, the harder it becomes. Avoid distractions and distracting situations. Outside noises and activities will compete for your attention if you let them. Keep the preview information in mind as you read. This will help to focus your attention on the selection.

2. Read in Thought Groups

Individual words do not tell us much. They must be combined with other words in order to yield meaning. To obtain meaning from the printed page, therefore, the reader should see the words in meaningful combinations. If you see only a word at a time (called word-by-word reading), your comprehension suffers along with your speed. To improve both speed and comprehension, try to group the words into phrases which have a natural relationship to each other. For practice, you might want to read aloud, trying to speak the words in meaningful combinations.

3. Question the Author

To sustain the pace you have set for yourself, and to maintain a high level of comprehension, question the writer as you read. Continually ask yourself such questions as, "What does this mean? What is he saying now? How can I use this information?" Questions like these help you to concentrate fully on the selection.

Steps to Faster Reading

**Step 3:
Grasp Paragraph Sense** *The paragraph is the basic unit of meaning. If you can discover quickly and understand the main point of each paragraph, you can comprehend the author's message. Good readers know how to find the main ideas of paragraphs quickly. This helps to make them faster readers.*

1. Find the Topic Sentence The topic sentence, the sentence containing the main idea, is often the first sentence of a paragraph. It is followed by other sentences which support, develop, or explain the main idea. Sometimes a topic sentence comes at the end of a paragraph. When it does, the supporting details come first, building the base for the topic sentence. Some paragraphs do not have a topic sentence. Such paragraphs usually create a mood or feeling, rather than present information.

2. Understand Paragraph Structure Every well-written paragraph has purpose. The purpose may be to inform, define, explain, persuade, compare or contrast, illustrate, and so on. The purpose should always relate to the main idea and expand on it. As you read each paragraph, see how the body of the paragraph is used to tell you more about the main idea or topic sentence. Read the supporting details intelligently, recognizing that what you are reading is all designed to develop the single main idea.

Steps to Faster Reading

**Step 4:
Organize Facts** *When you read, do you tend to see a lot of facts without any apparent connection or relationship? Understanding how the facts all fit together to deliver the author's message is, after all, the reason for reading. Good readers organize facts as they read. This helps them to read rapidly and well.*

1. Discover the Writer's Plan Look for a clue or signal word early in the article which might reveal the author's structure. Every writer has a plan or outline which he follows. If the reader can discover his method of organization, he has the key to understanding the message. Sometimes the author gives you obvious signals. If he says, "There are three reasons . . ." the wise reader looks for a listing of the three items. Other less obvious signal words such as *moreover, otherwise, consequently* all tell the reader the direction the writer's message will take.

2. Relate as You Read As you read the selection, keep the information learned during the preview in mind. See how the ideas you are reading all fit into place. Consciously strive to relate what you are reading to the title. See how the author is carrying through in his attempt to piece together a meaningful message. As you discover the relationship among the ideas, the message comes through quickly and clearly.

1. Let's Keep It Clean

Reading Time _____

Comprehension Score _____

Words per Minute _____

Did you ever stop to think how important water is? All animals and plants are mostly water. A person's body is about 65 percent water. Each of us needs to drink at least five pints of water each day. Big animals need about 15 gallons of water a day.

Water has other uses, too. It is used for washing and air conditioning. It is used for household work and gardening. Steel, gasoline, paper and most other products are made with the help of water. Power plants use water for cooling. Farms, of course, need water to grow food.

Water is even used to carry goods and people around the world. Water is used for swimming, boating and other kinds of recreation. Water is the home of many animals and plants, such as fish, whales, clams and seaweeds.

We can easily see that life would be impossible without water. That is why it is so important to keep our water clean and usuable. Yet, polluted water is becoming very common.

Water that has become polluted is unsafe to use. Pollution can happen when sewage and other untreated wastes have been dumped into it. Polluted water can smell, have garbage floating in it, and be unfit for swimming or boating. But even water that looks clean and smells good can be polluted. It may be loaded with germs and dangerous chemicals that you cannot see.

People pollute water in a lot of ways. One way is to allow bathroom and factory wastes to flow through pipes and into waterways without being treated. Another way is to allow soil, fertilizers and industrial wastes to wash from farms, building sites and mining sites into waterways after a rain.

Bacteria can feed on some wastes. Other wastes can be diluted by water in waterways. But nature can only do so much. Man is making more waste than nature can handle. More and better wastewater treatment is needed.

It is a fact that not all towns properly treat their drinking water. Many people think that the water they drink is safe. Most of the time it is. But about 4,000 Americans become sick each year by germs in unsafe drinking water. Many more cases are not reported.

Clean water is so important to our lives. We should make an effort to make sure we will have enough of it.

Selection 1: Recalling Facts

1. What percent of a person's body is water?
   ☐ a. 25 percent ☐ b. 50 percent ☐ c. 65 percent

2. Each of us needs at least five pints of water
   ☐ a. a day. ☐ b. a week. ☐ c. a month.

3. Water is used to make
   ☐ a. coal. ☐ b. gold. ☐ c. steel.

4. Power plants use water for
   ☐ a. boating. ☐ b. cooling. ☐ c. transportation.

5. About how many cases of illness caused by drinking unsafe water are reported each year in America?
   ☐ a. 2,000 ☐ b. 4,000 ☐ c. 10,000

Selection 1: Understanding Ideas

6. This article suggests that polluted water
   ☐ a. always looks dirty.
   ☐ b. carries many germs.
   ☐ c. is not very common.

7. This article is mostly about
   ☐ a. freshwater animals.
   ☐ b. the importance of water.
   ☐ c. popular waterways.

8. Polluted water
   ☐ a. always has an odor.
   ☐ b. is usually found near the ocean.
   ☐ c. sometimes looks safe and clean.

9. Water often becomes polluted because we allow
   ☐ a. oil barges to travel the waterways.
   ☐ b. people to swim and boat in clean water.
   ☐ c. untreated wastes to enter our waterways.

10. Which of the following can help keep our water clean?
    ☐ a. Stronger chemicals
    ☐ b. Treatment plants
    ☐ c. Wire fences

2. Drug Facts

Reading Time ————

Comprehension Score ————

Words per Minute ————

If often helps to know something about drugs. A drug is a chemical substance. It can bring about a physical, emotional or mental change in people. Alcohol and tobacco are drugs. The caffeine found in coffee, tea, cocoa, and cola drinks is a drug.

Drug abuse is the use of a drug, legal or illegal that hurts a person or someone close to him. A drug user is the person who takes the drug. There are many kinds of drug users. We have the experimental users. These people may try out drugs once or twice. They want to see what the effects will be. Recreational users take drugs to get high. They use drugs with friends or at parties to get into the mood of things. Regular users take drugs all the time. But they are able to keep up with the normal routine of work, school, housework, and so on. Dependent users can't relate to anything other than drugs. Their whole life centers around drugs. They feel extreme mental or real pain when they need drugs.

All drugs can be harmful. The effect of any drug depends on a lot of things. How a drug acts depends on how much or how often it is taken. It depends on the way it is taken. Some drugs are smoked. Others are swallowed or injected. Drugs act differently on different people. The place and the people around you affect the way a drug works.

Sometimes people take more than one drug. Multiple drug use is not only common, but also harmful. A deadly example is the use of alcohol and sleeping pills at the same time. Together these drugs can stop normal breathing and lead to death.

It is not always easy to tell if someone is on drugs. In the early stages, drug use is often hard to see. Sometimes people like drugs or need drugs so much they can't do without them. We say they are dependent. Only a few kinds of drugs, like the narcotics, can cause physical dependence. But almost any drug, when it is misused, can make you think you need it all the time. By this time it is too late and the person has been "hooked."

Tobacco, alcohol and marihuana are three very common drugs. These three are called the "gateway drugs." They are the first ones most people use and become dependent on.

Selection 2: Recalling Facts

1. A drug is a
   - ☐ a. chemical.
   - ☐ b. mineral.
   - ☐ c. vegetable.

2. The drug found in coffee and tea is called
   - ☐ a. alcohol.
   - ☐ b. caffeine.
   - ☐ c. marihuana.

3. People who take drugs at parties are called
   - ☐ a. dependent users.
   - ☐ b. experimental users.
   - ☐ c. recreational users.

4. When people can't do without drugs, we say they are
   - ☐ a. dependent.
   - ☐ b. independent.
   - ☐ c. misused.

5. Tobacco, alcohol and marihuana are called the
   - ☐ a. escape drugs.
   - ☐ b. gateway drugs.
   - ☐ c. service drugs.

Selection 2: Understanding Ideas

6. What is the main idea of this article?
   - ☐ a. Drug abuse is on the rise in America.
   - ☐ b. It helps to know something about drugs.
   - ☐ c. The use of marihuana should be made legal.

7. The writer makes this passage clear by using
   - ☐ a. facts.
   - ☐ b. numbers.
   - ☐ c. stories.

8. This passage hints that drug abuse can cause
   - ☐ a. hair loss.
   - ☐ b. physical pain.
   - ☐ c. sleeping sickness.

9. We can see that drugs
   - ☐ a. are made from herbs.
   - ☐ b. can be dangerous.
   - ☐ c. are easy to make.

10. Narcotics can cause
    - ☐ a. cold sores.
    - ☐ b. normal breathing.
    - ☐ c. physical dependence.

3. Cold Weather Care

Reading Time _____

Comprehension Score _____

Words per Minute _____

Enjoy the great outdoors, but be careful. People who are outside when it is very cold and windy tire quickly. Also, body heat is lost fast. If you must go outdoors, take extra care.

Cold weather itself, without any work on your part, puts an extra strain on the heart. If you add to this the strain of hard work, you are taking a risk. Hard work includes shoveling snow, pushing a stalled car, or even just walking too fast or too far.

If you do go out, be sure to dress warmly. Try to wear light wool clothes that do not fit too tightly. Outer garments should shed water. Wear a wool hat. Protect your face and cover your mouth to keep very cold air from your lungs. Wear mittens instead of gloves. They allow your fingers to move freely and will keep your hands warmer.

Watch out for frostbite and any other signs of danger from being in the cold too long. Frostbite causes a loss of feeling in the fingers, toes, tip of the nose, or ear lobes. These areas may become white or pale. If you see such signs, get help right away. Do not rub them with snow or ice. This treatment does not help and could make matters worse.

Do not drink alcohol when you are out in the cold. This makes you lose body heat even faster. You may feel warmer at first, but you will end up colder than before.

Try to keep your clothes and yourself dry. Change wet socks right away. Remove all wet clothing as soon as you can to stop loss of body heat. Wet clothes do not help you to keep in body heat.

If someone with you shows signs of illness from the cold, take action quickly. Even if someone claims to be all right, you should still act. Often the person will not realize how bad off he might be. Get the person into dry clothing and into a warm bed. Use a hot water bottle which should not be hot but warm to the touch. Use warm towels or a heating pad or any other source of heat to warm the bed. Put the heat on the trunk of the body first. Keep the head low and the feet up. Give the person warm drinks. If symptoms are very bad, call for a doctor right away.

Selection 3: Recalling Facts

1. People who go outside in very cold windy weather usually
   ☐ a. die.   ☐ b. get lost.   ☐ c. tire quickly.

2. Cold weather puts an extra strain on the
   ☐ a. brain.   ☐ b. heart.   ☐ c. kidneys.

3. In cold weather you should protect your face and mouth to keep cold air from your
   ☐ a. eyes.   ☐ b. lungs.   ☐ c. throat.

4. Frostbite causes a loss of
   ☐ a. feeling.   ☐ b. memory.   ☐ c. speech.

5. Alcohol makes you lose
   ☐ a. added weight.   ☐ b. body heat.   ☐ c. extra water.

Selection 3: Understanding Ideas

6. Being out in very cold weather can be
   ☐ a. dangerous.   ☐ b. fun.   ☐ c. helpful.

7. This article hints that
   ☐ a. alcohol warms the blood.
   ☐ b. wet clothes keep the body warm.
   ☐ c. wool clothes are warm.

8. We can see that frostbite
   ☐ a. does not require immediate attention.
   ☐ b. makes the skin very white.
   ☐ c. puts an extra strain on the heart.

9. If someone shows signs of illness from the cold, you should
   ☐ a. get that person to drink some alcohol.
   ☐ b. rub that person with snow or ice.
   ☐ c. try to keep the person warm.

10. Which of these would be a good title for this article?
    ☐ a. How to Handle Cold Weather
    ☐ b. Old Wives Tales
    ☐ c. Weather Patterns of the United States

4. Busy Little Carpenters

Reading Time _____

Comprehension Score _____

Words per Minute _____

Most people think of termites when they think of insects that live in wood. But there are other kinds of wood-nesting insects. Unlike termites, carpenter ants and carpenter bees do not eat wood. They simply nest in it. But they are still a problem because they can do a lot of damage while making their nests.

Carpenter ants are easy to spot. They are large and reddish-brown or black. Workers are from ¼ to ½ inch long. The workers have strong jaws and will bite when disturbed. Indoors the ants feed on sweets and other foods.

Colonies of carpenter ants are started by mated queens. The queen seeks damp wood for her nest. Once started, the nest is moved into dry, sound wood. The ants carve out their living quarters. They keep them clean and smooth. Sawdust from the nest is carried outside and dumped. If you see large ants around the house, beware! It is usually the first sign of a nest. The nest may not be inside, however. It may be in a stump or hollow tree near the house. But who knows when they might decide to move in.

Wood that has become damp should be watched carefully. Places that come under attack are porch pillars and supporting timbers. Other places to look are sills, joists, studs, and window and door trim. It is a good idea to poke the dampened wood with a sharp object. If the wood gives way and ants come tumbling out, the nest has likely been found.

Besides carpenter ants, there are carpenter bees. Carpenter bees look a lot like bumblebees. They range in size from ¼ to an inch long. Some are as large as bumblebees. However, carpenter bees have bare, shiny abdomens. The abdomens of bumblebees are covered with rows of thick yellow hair.

Carpenter bees cut an entrance hole across the grain of the wood. Then, they build their homes with the grain of the wood. They usually build their nests in dead twigs or branches. The damage caused by one or two bees is slight. But if they are not stopped, they can cause much damage over a long period.

By watching the bees, the nests can usually be found. It's a good idea to stop them before they spread and cause problems. The only good way to control pests is to poison their nests.

Selection 4: Recalling Facts

1. What color are carpenter ants?
   □ a. Dark gray and white
   □ b. Reddish-brown or black
   □ c. White and yellow

2. How big are carpenter ant workers?
   □ a. ¼ to ½ inch long   □ b. ½ to ¾ inch long   □ c. ¾ to 1 inch long

3. The queen carpenter ant makes her nest in
   □ a. cement walls.   □ b. damp wood.   □ c. old newspapers.

4. Carpenter bees look a lot like
   □ a. bumblebees.   □ b. hornets.   □ c. termites.

5. Carpenter bees have bare, shiny
   □ a. abdomens.   □ b. heads.   □ c. legs.

Selection 4: Understanding Ideas

6. Termites eat
   □ a. bees.   □ b. grass.   □ c. wood.

7. Carpenter ants and carpenter bees destroy wood by
   □ a. eating it.   □ b. nesting in it.   □ c. wetting it.

8. The head of the carpenter ant colony is the
   □ a. soldier.   □ b. queen.   □ c. worker.

9. We can see that carpenter ants keep their nests
   □ a. dirty and untidy.
   □ b. neat and clean.
   □ c. slimy and wet.

10. This article hints that carpenter ants and carpenter bees
    □ a. are helpful to man.
    □ b. fight each other.
    □ c. live in groups.

5. Safety First

Reading Time ———————

Comprehension Score ———————

Words per Minute ———————

There are many things around the house that can hurt a child. For example, baby's crib and playpen are not always safe. These things can sometimes be an area of great danger to an infant. You should take care when you buy such items. When choosing a crib or a playpen, be sure that the slats are spaced no more than two-and-one-half inches apart. With slats like this, the baby cannot catch his head between them. Be careful, too, of loose slats that could come out. A missing slat leaves a gap. The infant's head could easily get caught.

Even thin plastic, the kind you get from the cleaners, can be a very dangerous thing in a baby's world. It should never be used to cover a crib mattress. It should not be left where a baby could grab it and pull it over his face. A baby has no defense against this kind of thin, sticky plastic. The plastic can cling to his mouth and nose, cutting off his air supply.

We know that every home contains a great number of things that are tempting to a baby. These objects can do a lot of harm when baby is in the hand-to-mouth stage. Before putting a child down on the floor to play, check the floor carefully. Keep things like buttons, beads, pins, screws, or anything small out of baby's reach. Look out for anything small enough to fit in the infant's mouth. Small objects can get lodged in the throat and cut off the child's air supply.

Toys are not always safe either. The most dangerous toys for a child under three are those small enough to swallow. Do not let a young child play with marbles or small plastic toys. Avoid toys which come apart easily. Do not buy stuffed animals or dolls with tiny button eyes or ornaments that can be easily pulled off. Never let a child chew on balloons. He might bite off a piece and choke.

Do not feed a young child popcorn, nuts, or small, hard candies. Doctors find that young children do not know how to eat things like these. These foods can easily get sucked into the windpipe instead of going to the stomach. The same is true of pills. Use liquid medicine. If pills must be used, they should be crushed.

Selection 5: Recalling Facts

1. The slats of a crib or playpen should be spaced no more than
   - ☐ a. 2½ inches apart.
   - ☐ b. 5 inches apart.
   - ☐ c. 5½ inches apart.

2. Which of the following should never be used to cover a crib mattress?
   - ☐ a. Linen sheets   ☐ b. Thin plastic   ☐ c. Woolen blankets

3. You should not buy stuffed animals that have
   - ☐ a. colored ribbons.   ☐ b. large feet.   ☐ c. tiny button eyes.

4. Which of the following toys might prove dangerous to a small child?
   - ☐ a. Balloons   ☐ b. Rattles   ☐ c. Puppets

5. A young child should not be allowed to eat
   - ☐ a. bread.   ☐ b. spaghetti.   ☐ c. nuts.

Selection 5: Understanding Ideas

6. What is the main thought of this article?
   - ☐ a. Children learn how to walk before they run.
   - ☐ b. Doctors know that children do not know how to eat popcorn.
   - ☐ c. Some things around the house are harmful to children.

7. We can see that young children like to
   - ☐ a. cry a lot before they go to bed.
   - ☐ b. put things in their mouths.
   - ☐ c. have temper tantrums.

8. Thin plastic can cause a baby
   - ☐ a. to sleep.   ☐ b. to smile.   ☐ c. to smother.

9. Hard candies can make a child
   - ☐ a. breathe.   ☐ b. choke.   ☐ c. whine.

10. For a child, swallowing liquid medicine is easier than swallowing
    - ☐ a. pills.   ☐ b. syrup.   ☐ c. water.

6. Happy Birthday to You

What do the candles on your birthday cake mean? They simply tell your age. That's all. They don't tell what kind of jobs you can do. They don't say how healthy you are. Yet, your age has become a figure that can control your life. Your income, your social benefits, your way of life greatly depend upon your age.

Yet a person's "calendar" age may not be a good measurement to use. You may be sixty-five years old by the calendar. Still you may feel and act even younger than a person who is fifty-five.

As a result, employers today are starting to depend more on "functional" age. The actual date of birth is becoming less of a factor. An older worker has a great deal to offer his company. He is wiser, more experienced and uses better judgment than new employees. As a rule, he knows how to make a decision and when to make it. He knows when to speak up and when not to. Most important, he probably knows when to listen, something that is usually not seen before middle age.

Even the idea of middle age may change, too. People are living longer. People may soon be living to ages well over 100. When this happens, middle age would then be placed at seventy. Since our country is faced with shortages of many goods and services, we should start to think of a person's ability to contribute, regardless of age.

History tells us of people who reached their peak after middle age. Verdi wrote "Othello" when he was seventy-three. Cervantes wrote *Don Quixote* when in his middle years. Ben Franklin invented bifocal lenses when he was in his seventies.

Pearl Buck, a great writer, once talked about her eightieth birthday. She said that she was a far better person at eighty than she was at fifty or forty. She said that she had learned a great deal since she was seventy. She felt that she had learned more in those ten years than in any other ten-year period.

In fact, Pearl was right. Studies show that smart people tend to get smarter as they grow older. The brain is like a muscle. The more you use it, the more it develops. Each one of us has something that can be used to help society and ourselves. Let's not let the candles on a birthday cake stand in the way.

Selection 6: Recalling Facts

1. Your age controls your
   ☐ a. family.   ☐ b. friends.   ☐ c. income.

2. When people start to live to be over 100 years old, middle age will be
   ☐ a. fifty.   ☐ b. sixty.   ☐ c. seventy.

3. Who wrote "Othello"?
   ☐ a. Cervantes   ☐ b. Plato   ☐ c. Verdi

4. Franklin invented bifocal lenses when he was in his
   ☐ a. forties.   ☐ b. fifties.   ☐ c. seventies.

5. Pearl Buck was a famous
   ☐ a. doctor.   ☐ b. lawyer.   ☐ c. writer.

Selection 6: Understanding Ideas

6. What would be another good title for this article?
   ☐ a. Famous Scientists in History
   ☐ b. The History of Birthday Cakes
   ☐ c. You Don't Act Your Age

7. What is the main idea of this article?
   ☐ a. Some older people have interesting hobbies.
   ☐ b. Many older people act younger than their ages.
   ☐ c. Most older people retire when they reach sixty-five.

8. Employers are finding out that older workers are
   ☐ a. good for the company.
   ☐ b. poor decision makers.
   ☐ c. quite sickly.

9. We can see that many people invent things
   ☐ a. after their middle years.
   ☐ b. before they go to college.
   ☐ c. quite often by accident.

10. The older you get,
    ☐ a. the happier you become.
    ☐ b. the shorter you become.
    ☐ c. the smarter you become.

7. Castles in the Air

Reading Time _____

Comprehension Score _____

Words per Minute _____

Life during the Middle Ages was hard. People were always at war. Therefore, castles were built to protect people from their enemies.

The castle was the home of a lord and his family. It was also the home of the soldiers. The soldiers were there to protect the castle, the lord and his family. They also protected the village from attack. The castle was also the prison and the treasure house. It was even the center of local government.

Most castles were built on a hill or high ground. This made the castle easy to defend. A moat (a deep ditch filled with water) was built around the castle. A drawbridge, which could be raised and lowered with winches and chains, lay across the moat.

During the Middle Ages, most castles were built in the shape of a square. They had a large tower in each corner. These towers were usually made of stone. A thick stone wall ran from tower to tower and formed an area called the inner ward. A large central tower was called the keep. This was always the very strongest part of the castle. The lord and his family lived on the upper floors of the keep. The soldiers lived on the lower levels. The keep had many secret rooms and getaway passages. It was here, in the keep, that all the village people would hide during times of great danger. There were many underground tunnels leading to the keep. The other towers were used for the prison. The great hall was the place for town meetings. The kitchen and bake shop were also part of the castle.

The space outside the towers and wall was called the outer ward. This outer ward was surrounded by another wall. This second wall also ran around the whole village. The top of this wall had a walk for the soldiers and battlements (high stone shields). From behind the battlements the soldiers could hide and shoot their arrows and cast stones at the enemy.

At the end of the Middle Ages, castles disappeared. They were replaced by forts. But many rich homes, homes of lords and earls, were still built in the shape of a castle. Castles have always held the interest of people. Even today in European countries the old romantic castles are a big tourist attraction. Many people flock to see these buildings of time.

Selection 7: Recalling Facts

1. Castles were used to protect people from their
   □ a. enemies. □ b. friends. □ c. pets.

2. The castle was also a
   □ a. church. □ b. market. □ c. prison.

3. Most castles were built on a
   □ a. cliff. □ b. hill. □ c. lake.

4. The ditch filled with water that surrounded the castle was called a
   □ a. crevice. □ b. keep. □ c. moat.

5. Battlements are high stone
   □ a. shields. □ b. statues. □ c. walls.

Selection 7: Understanding Ideas

6. People during the Middle Ages were
   □ a. friendly. □ b. poetic. □ c. warlike.

7. We can see that castles were
   □ a. small shacks.
   □ b. sturdy buildings.
   □ c. tiny caves.

8. If a friend wished to enter the castle, the drawbridge had to be
   □ a. destroyed. □ b. lowered. □ c. raised.

9. This article hints that castles were mostly made of
   □ a. stone. □ b. straw. □ c. wood.

10. Getaway passages were probably used when people wanted to
    □ a. escape. □ b. fight. □ c. vacation.

8. An Indian Hero

Black Hawk was a Sauk Indian who hated the white settlers. For years, the Sauk and Fox Indians hunted and fished in what is now Illinois and Wisconsin. Soon, white settlers pushed into the land. Under a treaty, the land was taken from the Indians by the settlers.

From boyhood Black Hawk learned to hate the white man. His fame as a fearless warrior began at age 15 when he killed and scalped his first man. Black Hawk went on to fight. First he fought enemy Indian tribes. Later he fought the white man.

Above all else, Black Hawk hated the 1804 treaty which had taken away Sauk and Fox lands. He spoke against the treaty. He called it unfair since the Indians who had signed it were tricked into agreeing to its terms. Black Hawk believed that Indian land could not be sold. He was determined to stay and farm the land.

Black Hawk and his followers refused to leave their villages. By 1831, the Indians found themselves unable to farm their own lands. Black Hawk ordered the whites to get out or be killed. Instead, soldiers moved in and threw the Indians off the land.

Black Hawk felt that he could band together enough Indians to fight the white man. He set out to ask help from other tribes. In April 1832, Black Hawk and several hundred warriors returned to Illinois. He was ready to drive the whites from Indian land. The fighting known as "Black Hawk's War" began. Soon troops from Washington were sent into the field to put down the Indians. For 3 months the Indians managed to escape the troops. They won several small battles and were raiding the Illinois frontier.

The tide turned as more soldiers poured in. The troops chased the Indians from Illinois to Mississippi. There, Black Hawk was trapped. He faced the steamship Warrior on one side and the army on the other. Black Hawk's band was nearly destroyed. The Sauk leader himself escaped to a Winnebago village. There he gave himself up and was taken to a prison camp in chains. A few months later he was set free.

In 1838, at the age of 71, Black Hawk died in his lodge on the Des Moines River. As he wished, Black Hawk's body was seated on the ground under a wooden shelter, in old Sauk tradition.

Selection 8: Recalling Facts

1. Black Hawk was a
   ☐ a. Fox Indian.   ☐ b. Sauk Indian.   ☐ c. Sioux Indian.

2. Black Hawk's fame as a warrior began when he was
   ☐ a. 10.   ☐ b. 15.   ☐ c. 20.

3. Black Hawk
   ☐ a. hated the 1804 treaty.
   ☐ b. liked the 1804 treaty.
   ☐ c. signed the 1804 treaty.

4. The soldiers chased Black Hawk from Illinois to
   ☐ a. Florida.   ☐ b. Mississippi.   ☐ c. Texas.

5. Black Hawk died at the age of
   ☐ a. 65.   ☐ b. 71.   c. 82.

Selection 8: Understanding Ideas

6. Black Hawk lived in
   ☐ a. New England.
   ☐ b. the Midwest.
   ☐ c. the deep South.

7. We can see that at times
   ☐ a. the Indians grew tasty corn.
   ☐ b. Indian tribes fought each other.
   ☐ c. white settlers traveled in wagons.

8. This article hints that the white man treated the Indians
   ☐ a. kindly.
   ☐ b. respectfully.
   ☐ c. unfairly.

9. The Sauk Indians were mostly
   ☐ a. farmers.   ☐ b. fishermen.   ☐ c. hunters.

10. How long did it take Black Hawk to gather his Indian warriors?
    ☐ a. One year   ☐ b. Two years   ☐ c. Three years

9. A Guided Tour

Reading Time _____

Comprehension Score _____

Words per Minute _____

Do you plan to visit Italy someday? If so, it's a good idea to know about the country and its people. Italy has two very different areas. The business centers and large cities of the North hum with noise. The South, on the other hand, enjoys the sleepy charm of the country. People of the North like the bustle of city life. They enjoy all the things a city has to offer. Those from the South like a slower pace. They like their rural surroundings. One thing all Italians have in common is their zest for life.

The climate of Italy is like that of California. It is sunny and warm all year in the South. Except in the mountains, summers are warm all over the country. Winter brings snow, sleet, cold rain and fog to the North. Central Italy is mild in winter.

Many Italians are happiest when in groups. Wherever they gather, you are likely to hear fine singing and happy laughter.

A building boom is going on in the cities of Italy. Steel and glass skyscrapers tower over ancient ruins. Italy throbs with life and color. Talk on the street corners is lively. The background music coming from open windows could be classical or the latest hit tune. Donkeys and street peddlers sometimes add to the color and noise.

The city streets are busy. Here you will see well-dressed people. These people are going to work in new office buildings. The street traffic includes different kinds of cars. You can even spot some motor scooters and bicycles.

Italians also like food. They are good cooks. Each city and region has its own specialties. Bologna, for instance, is known for its sausages. Olive oil, garlic and tomatoes are used more freely in cooking in the South than in the North. Some Northerners use butter instead of olive oil. You will see rice on their plates instead of pasta.

An Italian dinner begins with appetizers and ends many courses later with a fine dessert. In the course of a dinner, you can sample some of Italy's fine cheeses. There are many to choose from. There are also many fine wines, and they are reasonably priced.

You may never visit Italy. Still, it's nice to read about its lively and colorful personality. Maybe someday you will be lucky enough to see part of this wonderful land.

Selection 9: Recalling Facts

1. The business areas of Italy are found in the
   - ☐ a. East.
   - ☐ b. North.
   - ☐ c. South.

2. Even though Italians differ slightly, they all love
   - ☐ a. life.
   - ☐ b. money.
   - ☐ c. wine.

3. The climate of Italy is like that of
   - ☐ a. California.
   - ☐ b. Mississippi.
   - ☐ c. New York.

4. Central Italy is mild during the
   - ☐ a. spring.
   - ☐ b. summer.
   - ☐ c. winter.

5. Which of the following adds to the color and noise of Italy?
   - ☐ a. Roving circuses
   - ☐ b. Street peddlers
   - ☐ c. Wildlife

Selection 9: Understanding Ideas

6. The life styles of Northern and Southern Italy are
   - ☐ a. exactly the same.
   - ☐ b. quite similar.
   - ☐ c. very different.

7. The southern part of Italy is mostly
   - ☐ a. country.
   - ☐ b. desert.
   - ☐ c. swamp.

8. Southern Italy has warmer weather than
   - ☐ a. Central Italy.
   - ☐ b. Eastern Italy.
   - ☐ c. Northern Italy.

9. Most Italians are
   - ☐ a. gay and happy.
   - ☐ b. sly and calm.
   - ☐ c. quiet and sad.

10. Italian streets are
    - ☐ a. dangerous.
    - ☐ b. noisy.
    - ☐ c. quiet.

10. Vitamins at Work

Reading Time _____

Comprehension Score _____

Words per Minute _____

Vitamins are important to our bodies. They keep our bodies healthy. They help our bodies to grow. There are at least 25 different vitamins we know of. Each one has its own special use. The best way to get vitamins is to eat foods rich in them. It's a good idea, then, to know about foods and the vitamins they contain. Let's take a look at some special vitamins. We can start with vitamin A.

Vitamin A is needed for good eyesight. It helps us to see better at night. It even keeps our eyes free from disease. Vitamin A also keeps the skin healthy and stops infection. This vitamin is found in animal foods. However, deep yellow and dark green vegetables and fruits give our bodies something called "carotene." Our bodies can turn carotene into vitamin A.

Produce can easily supply all the vitamin A you need. Such items as collards, turnip greens, kale, carrots, squash and sweet potatoes can more than take care of daily needs. Yellow peaches, apricots, cantalope and papayas also help.

Liver is another good source of vitamin A. A two-ounce serving of cooked beef liver gives us more than 30,000 units of the vitamin. That's six times more vitamin A than you would need during the day.

There are plenty of other sources of vitamin A. Whole milk is a source. Skim milk, on the other hand, doesn't have any vitamin A, unless it is fortified. This means that vitamin A has been added to it.

Three of the best known vitamins come from the vitamin B complex. They are riboflavin, thiamin and niacin. These vitamins release the energy in food. They keep the nervous system working. They keep the digestive system working calmly. And they even help to keep the skin healthy.

Riboflavin is easy to find. It is found in meats, milk, and whole grain or enriched breads. Organ meats also have riboflavin.

Thiamin is found in few foods. Lean pork is one. Dry beans and peas and some of the organ meats give us some thiamin.

Niacin can be found in whole grain and enriched cereals. Meat and meat products and peas and beans also contain niacin. Without niacin, riboflavin and thiamin could not do their work properly.

Vitamins are important to a healthy body. It would pay us to learn more about these amazing building blocks.

Selection 10: Recalling Facts

1. Vitamins help keep our bodies
   - ☐ a. healthy.
   - ☐ b. tan.
   - ☐ c. weak.

2. Vitamin A is needed for good
   - ☐ a. bones.
   - ☐ b. energy.
   - ☐ c. eyesight.

3. Deep yellow and dark green vegetables give our bodies
   - ☐ a. calcium.
   - ☐ b. carotene.
   - ☐ c. fat.

4. Which of the following is a good source of vitamin A?
   - ☐ a. Liver
   - ☐ b. Sugar
   - ☐ c. Water

5. Thiamin is found in
   - ☐ a. enriched cereals.
   - ☐ b. lean pork.
   - ☐ c. whole milk.

Selection 10: Understanding Ideas

6. What is this article mostly about?
   - ☐ a. Fats, protein, sugar and starches
   - ☐ b. Vitamins A, B, C and D
   - ☐ c. Vitamin A, riboflavin, thiamin and niacin

7. To help us see better at night, we should eat
   - ☐ a. cabbage.
   - ☐ b. candy.
   - ☐ c. squash.

8. About how many units of vitamin A do we need a day?
   - ☐ a. 1,000
   - ☐ b. 5,000
   - ☐ c. 30,000

9. Some organ meats are rich in vitamin A and
   - ☐ a. calcium.
   - ☐ b. riboflavin.
   - ☐ c. vitamin K.

10. This article suggests that riboflavin, thiamin and niacin
    - ☐ a. build bones.
    - ☐ b. tone muscles.
    - ☐ c. work together.

11. A Toast to the Toaster

Reading Time _____

Comprehension Score _____

Words per Minute _____

Electric toasters have come a long way since the 1920s. Today, you can even choose the color of your toast. Modern toasters even shut off by themselves. Some models can also warm and bake. Toasters come in two styles. They are either upright or horizontal types. The upright toasters hold the bread in an up-and-down position. In the horizontal type, the slices lie flat.

There are two kinds of upright toasters. The first type holds two or four slices of bread. Other upright models have ovens. These ovens can toast, warm or bake.

The first kind of upright toaster has often been called an automatic pop-up toaster. Some people even call them wall toasters. They toast bread, frozen waffles, and thin pastries without toppings or fillings. They are simple machines and are easy to work. The bread carriage has an outside control knob. When the knob is worked, the carriage moves up and down inside the toast wells. The carriage works an on-off switch. The heating elements in an upright toaster are made of fine wires. These are placed on both sides of each toast well. When electricity flows through the wires, they give off heat for toasting. A thermostat inside the toaster is hooked up to an outside toast-color control. The control lets you choose the toasting time.

The second upright model is both a toaster and a small oven. These models have toast wells, bread carriages, and toast-color controls. Plus, they have special doors and controls for baking and warming.

Horizontal toasters are either reflector models or toaster ovens. Reflector models toast and warm. Toaster ovens toast, warm and bake. Both have built-in two and four slice sizes and have a front door or opening. Both can handle most bread sizes.

Choose your toaster carefully. Look for a seal of approval from an independent testing laboratory. This seal is important. It lets you know that this toaster is as safe as possible. The seal might be on the toaster. It may also be on the packing carton. Such a seal shows, among other things, that the toaster has a two-pole switch. This switch is a safety point. It stops a child from getting a shock. Even if a child puts his hand inside the toasting chamber while the toaster is plugged in, he should not get a shock.

The next time you're in the market for a toaster, look for the seal of safety.

Selection 11: Recalling Facts

1. Electric toasters have come a long way since the
    ☐ a. 1860s.   ☐ b. 1880s.   ☐ c. 1920s.

2. Some toasters can warm and
    ☐ a. bake.   ☐ b. broil.   ☐ c. fry.

3. The heating elements in a toaster are made of fine
    ☐ a. screws.   ☐ b. threads.   ☐ c. wires.

4. Horizontal toasters are either reflector models or
    ☐ a. control toasters.
    ☐ b. pop-up broilers.
    ☐ c. toaster ovens.

5. A two-pole switch on a toaster stops a child from getting a
    ☐ a. burn.   ☐ b. cut.   ☐ c. shock.

Selection 11: Understanding Ideas

6. Toasters
    ☐ a. come in different styles.
    ☐ b. have not changed since 1900.
    ☐ c. serve one person at a time.

7. The pop-up toaster is also called a
    ☐ a. camp toaster.   ☐ b. serving toaster.   ☐ c. wall toaster.

8. In order to toast a piece of bread, you need
    ☐ a. heat.   ☐ b. sugar.   ☐ c. water.

9. A thermostat controls the
    ☐ a. color of the toast.
    ☐ b. size of the toast.
    ☐ c. weight of the toast.

10. How many types of horizontal toasters are there?
    ☐ a. One   ☐ b. Two   ☐ c. Three

12. The Right Choice

Fresh or frozen, canned or dried, instant or from scratch? Which foods have the nutrients? Which do not? The fact is they all do. All foods have their place. And almost all food in its place is good food. Some foods are safer to use when they are processed. Some are more appealing when they are fresh. It's a good idea to know your foods.

Packaged, pasteurized, fortified milk has been around for so long that no one thinks of it any more as a processed food, but it is. Because milk is pasteurized, or processed, it is now safe to drink. Unpasteurized milk may carry many germs that can make us sick.

Buy the mix or do it yourself? It is all the same nutritionally if the ingredients listed on the label are used in the same amounts and are the same ones as you would use doing it yourself.

Which bread is the best? Whole grain breads and cereals retain the germ and outer layers of grain where the B vitamins are. When wheat is milled into white flour, however, it loses these precious vitamins. Therefore, when you buy white bread, it is wise to choose the enriched kind because of added nutrients.

Fresh or frozen? Foods in the frozen food case offer as much food value as those in the produce section of the store. The choice you make depends on which foods you prefer and the amount of money you want to spend. Any loss of vitamin C in frozen fruits is minimal. Well-packaged frozen meat, poultry and fish are nutritious. They have the same food value as those that are bought right from the butcher or the fish store.

Surprisingly, fresh or raw foods are not always better than canned or frozen ones. It depends on how they are handled. For instance, leafy, dark green vegetables packed in crushed ice keep a lot of their vitamin C on the way to the store. But if they are left to sit for five days or so, they lose about half of it. Cooking will also cause some vitamin loss. Although the loss may be great, these vegetables contain large amounts of vitamins. They still provide good amounts of vitamin C and vitamin A when they are eaten.

Choosing the proper food is no game. It is a serious matter and one that we should pay much attention to.

Selection 12: Recalling Facts

1. Unpasteurized milk may carry many
   □ a. chemicals. □ b. germs. □ c. vitamins.

2. Enriched bread has added
   □ a. color. □ b. flavor. □ c. nutrients.

3. Frozen fruits lose only a small amount of
   □ a. vitamin A. □ b. vitamin B. □ c. vitamin C.

4. Frozen meat is nutritious as long as it is properly
   □ a. aged. □ b. packaged. □ c. stored.

5. Fresh vegetables lose some of their vitamins when they are
   □ a. cooked. □ b. packed. □ c. pickled.

Selection 12: Understanding Ideas

6. What is this article mostly about?
   □ a. Good food
   □ b. Junk food
   □ c. Poisoned food

7. Processing a food may make it
   □ a. less expensive.
   □ b. more filling.
   □ c. safer to eat.

8. Milk is
   □ a. a long-lasting food.
   □ b. a processed food.
   □ c. an unpackaged food.

9. Whole grain breads are more nutritious than
   □ a. frozen fish and meat.
   □ b. store-bought mixes.
   □ c. white milled wheat.

10. We can see that fresh and frozen foods have
    □ a. many kinds of germs.
    □ b. little vitamin C.
    □ c. the same food value.

13. Busy Blenders

Busy Blenders

The blender is one of the most useful kitchen tools. Its blades are sharp, small and turn at top speeds. Because of this, it can do many jobs. Blenders chop nuts, cheese, and pieces of vegetables. They crumble bread and crackers. They can puree cooked foods. They can even puree some fresh fruits and vegetables. Of course, they are used for blending spreads, dips, dressings and beverages. A blender with strong enough blades and container and a high wattage can even crush ice.

Most blenders use from 350 to 1,200 watts. If you buy a blender with a high wattage, be sure not to use it on the same circuit with other appliances. You could easily blow a fuse.

The speed controls on most blenders are pushbuttons. Most have an "off" setting for safety. Some models have as many as 20 speed buttons. Others have only high and low settings. The motor parts on blenders should already be oiled when you buy them. They are oiled in such a way that you never need to oil them again. Outside of soap-and-water cleaning, the blender needs very little home care.

The blades of your blender should be made of stainless steel. If they are not stainless steel, the blades might rust. The blades plus the base cap should come apart to make it easier for you to remove thick foods. This feature lets you wash and dry both the blades and the container thoroughly.

The container should have a pouring lip and a comfortable handle. It should fit firmly onto the blender base. Sometimes clear cup containers have measure markings on them. These markings are helpful. They cut out extra measuring steps as you follow a recipe. This saves you time.

The container lid should fit tightly. It should have a small removable cap. This little cap lets you add things to the container while the blender is running.

The base of the blender should be heavy. It should also be firm. The base should have rubber feet to stop the blender from sliding while it is on. The blades of a blender can be dangerous. Therefore, it's a good idea to learn a few safety rules.

Keep fingers and utensils away from blades. If anything drops into the blender, turn off the power at once. Before you remove the blender container, be sure that the blades have stopped completely.

Selection 13: Recalling Facts

1. A blender with strong enough blades can crush
   □ a. ice. □ b. metal. □ c. rock.

2. How many watts do most blenders use?
   □ a. 100−150 watts □ b. 350−1,200 watts □ c. 750−1,500 watts

3. If you use a high wattage blender on the same circuit with other appliances, you may
   □ a. blow a fuse. □ b. cause a flood. □ c. start a fire.

4. The speed controls on most blenders are
   □ a. dials. □ b. pushbuttons. □ c. switches.

5. The blades of a blender should be made of
   □ a. iron. □ b. hard plastic. □ c. stainless steel.

Selection 13: Understanding Ideas

6. Blenders are used to prepare
   □ a. foods. □ b. lessons. □ c. paints.

7. Some blenders have many different
   □ a. containers. □ b. lids. □ c. speeds.

8. Stainless steel does not
   □ a. dent. □ b. shine. □ c. rust.

9. This article hints that liquids
   □ a. can be easily poured from the blender's container.
   □ b. damage and finally destroy the blender.
   □ c. cannot be measured in a blender.

10. The blades of a blender can
    □ a. dent the container.
    □ b. harm a person.
    □ c. start a fire.

14. A Major Concern

Reading Time _____

Comprehension Score _____

Words per Minute _____

There is good reason to be concerned with the eating habits of teenagers. During the teen years, good food habits may be lost. The teenage appetite is often big. But a large appetite doesn't always mean much. Even with a big appetite, teenagers may not get the good foods they need. Teenage boys and girls grow at a fast rate. Except for infancy, the growth is faster than at any other time. A boy has great nutritional needs during the teen years. His needs are greater than at any other time in his life. The needs of a girl becoming a woman are great. Only during pregnancy and the period following the birth are they greater.

A teenage boy may suddenly shoot up as much as four inches in height. He may gain fifteen pounds a year. A teenage girl's total gain is not quite as large, but it is considerable. Growth means more than adding inches and weight. It means that body fat is lost while bones increase in density. Muscles develop in size and strength.

Teenage eating habits are often bad. The reasons are not hard to find. School, clubs and part-time jobs keep teenagers away from home at mealtime. Their eating habits are influenced more by friends than by parents. Some skip breakfast because they don't have enough time for it. Some choose snacks that are too rich in fats and sugar. Teenage girls sometimes eat too little because they do not want to get fat. Diets have to be well planned for both boys and girls. Each has a great need for protein and vitamins. The need is so great that they cannot afford to fill up on foods that have empty calories. Most of the time a teenage boy winds up with a better diet than a girl. This happens simply because the boy has a bigger appetite and eats more. But some boys may shy away from foods that have important nutrients. Instead, they may eat great amounts of junk food. Sometimes this creates a weight problem.

The overweight teenager may eat the same kinds of food as his average friend, but too much of them. Rich desserts and snack foods should be replaced with fresh fruits and vegetables.

Instead of a crash diet to take off pounds, overweight teenagers should develop the well-balanced eating habits they need for the rest of their lives.

Selection 14: Recalling Facts

1. The teenager has a big
   □ a. appetite.   □ b. stomach.   □ c. voice.

2. The growth rate during the teen years is not as rapid as it is during
   □ a. infancy.   □ b. puberty.   □ c. adolescence.

3. Each year, a teenage boy may gain as much as
   □ a. two pounds.   □ b. five pounds.   □ c. fifteen pounds.

4. Who has the most influence on teenage eating habits?
   □ a. Doctors   □ b. Friends   □ c. Parents

5. Some teenagers choose snacks that are too rich in fats and
   □ a. minerals.   □ b. protein.   □ c. sugar.

Selection 14: Understanding Ideas

6. During the teen years, good food habits often
   □ a. develop.   □ b. disappear.   □ c. remain.

7. This article hints that teenagers
   □ a. choose good foods.
   □ b. grow very fast.
   □ c. like loud sounds.

8. We can see that during the teen years
   □ a. bones and muscles get stronger.
   □ b. growing bones break easily.
   □ c. many boys and girls become ill.

9. Teenagers seem to be very
   □ a. active.   □ b. lazy.   □ c. sad.

10. Teenage girls do not want to
    □ a. get a job.   □ b. grow taller.   □ c. gain weight.

15. Mix It Up

A mixer in the kitchen can speed up your work. It can make your work easier. This wonderful invention can stir sauces and gravies. A mixer can mash potatoes. It can cream sugar and shortening. And, of course, a mixer can mix batters. Mixers come in three styles: portable, stand and convertible.

The portable mixer is held in your hand. You direct the pair of beaters around a pan or bowl. This type of mixer has a light-duty electric motor. It uses from 100 to 150 watts of current. It is mainly used to stir thin batters. Models with higher wattage can stir thicker mixtures. A portable mixer can be used to make packaged cakes, puddings and gelatin. It is useful for whipping cream and beating eggs. And, it is easy to store. It can be kept in a drawer or hung on a wall.

Unlike the portable mixer, the stand mixer has a rather heavy frame with the mixer head at the top. There is a wide base big enough for large bowls or a bowl turntable. To make sure that things get mixed properly, the beaters usually turn the bowl and turntable as they mix. Some stand mixers use from 200 to 400 watts of electricity. Those with high ratings can mix thick batters and mix bread dough. Because of their size and weight, stand mixers are usually left in place on a kitchen counter.

The convertible mixer is similar to the stand type mixer except that the head can be removed for portable use or storage. Heads of heavy-duty models, however, may be tiring to hold.

On all mixers, speed control switches or dials should be well located. They should be easy to read. They should have an "off" setting for safety. Some mixer controls only have settings for high, medium or low speeds. Other mixers have speed controls that have a better range.

Some mixers have extra attachments or parts you can buy. For instance, bowl sets, plastic beaters for non-stick pans and hooks for mixing dough are all extras. You can get wire whisk beaters for whipping and flat beaters for creaming. Some of these things may be added at no extra cost when you buy your mixer. Other attachments may have to be bought separately.

Almost all attachments have one thing in common—they make kitchen work a little easier.

Selection 15: Recalling Facts

1. A mixer can cream sugar and
   □ a. eggs. □ b. flour. □ c. shortening.

2. How many types of mixers are there?
   □ a. Three □ b. Four □ c. Five

3. A portable mixer is mainly used to stir
   □ a. bread dough.
   □ b. thick batters.
   □ c. thin batters.

4. The stand mixer has a heavy
   □ a. cord. □ b. frame. □ c. handle.

5. How much electricity does a stand mixer use?
   □ a. 50−100 watts □ b. 100−150 watts □ c. 200−400 watts

Selection 15: Understanding Ideas

6. Choose the best title for this article.
   □ a. Different Kinds of Mixers
   □ b. Electricity Makes the Difference
   □ c. Tasty Desserts

7. The portable mixer is probably
   □ a. dangerous. □ b. lightweight. □ c. pretty.

8. The stand mixer is not easy to
   □ a. sell. □ b. store. □ c. use.

9. The convertible mixer and the stand mixer are
   □ a. expensive. □ b. rustproof. □ c. similar.

10. Many mixers have
    □ a. extra parts. □ b. guide plates. □ c. sharp edges.

16. Moving Along with the Times

Reading Time _____

Comprehension Score _____

Words per Minute _____

Moving from one home to another can be a problem. If your new house is empty, it may seem as cold and as lifeless as a tomb. However, little by little you get settled. Your furniture arrives. Your clothes fill the closets. Before you know it, you look around and realize that all is in order. Moving wasn't so bad after all.

As a matter of fact, most people seem to enjoy it. Moving is one of the most widely shared adventures of our way of life. Long before the pioneers headed for the West, restlessness had been part of our nature. Today, it shows itself up and down and across the land as 40 million Americans change their homes every year.

Today, those who make long distance moves fall into one of three classes. Some are skilled workers who are seeking better jobs. Others are in military or government service and have been assigned to new posts.

The third class of mover shows the changing pattern of business life. About four out of ten long-distance moves are the result of job transfers. These are usually young businessmen who are often moved from one office to another. Some businessmen move as often as every two years.

Today, a long distance move need not be unpleasant. Just be sure you plan well. In fact, it could be nothing more than a short break in the daily routine. Moving companies now have trained people with years of experience. They know how to ship all kind of things. They can even handle fine art and antiques. Valuable instruments can be shipped without a scratch.

Damage to household goods in packing or on route is no longer a real problem. New ways for crating, packing and shipping have been found. For instance, some movers now use self-adjusting cartons for things like china and glasses. These cartons keep your glassware safe. Also, some companies use stuffing and plastic wrapping materials to protect delicate items.

On the way, the shipment is in the hands of drivers who are considered the best in the world today. The drivers of household moving vans are selected as the cream of the crop. They travel an average of 60,000 to 100,000 miles a year. That's a lot of miles. And it's a lot of experience. Moving is not so bad when you know you have skilled movers to help you.

Selection 16: Recalling Facts

1. How many Americans change their home each year?
   - □ a. 10 million
   - □ b. 20 million
   - □ c. 40 million

2. Skilled workers often move to find better
   - □ a. weather.
   - □ b. jobs.
   - □ c. schools.

3. About four out of ten long-distance moves are the result of
   - □ a. larger families.
   - □ b. poor health.
   - □ c. job transfers.

4. Which of the following is used to protect glassware items?
   - □ a. Metal racks
   - □ b. Self-adjusting cartons
   - □ c. Sturdy wooden crates

5. The drivers of household vans are well
   - □ a. educated.
   - □ b. paid.
   - □ c. selected.

Selection 16: Understanding Ideas

6. An empty house may seem
   - □ a. lifelike.
   - □ b. lifeless.
   - □ c. lively.

7. This article hints that a lot of people
   - □ a. hate to move.
   - □ b. like to move.
   - □ c. never move.

8. Young businessmen
   - □ a. are well schooled.
   - □ b. have large families.
   - □ c. move a lot.

9. We can see that
   - □ a. a well-planned move is not unpleasant.
   - □ b. moving from one place to another is difficult.
   - □ c. movers make a good salary each year.

10. Foam stuffing helps to protect your delicate items from
    - □ a. breaking.
    - □ b. freezing.
    - □ c. melting.

17. A Good Start

A child grows faster during the first few years of his life than at any other time. Thus, good nutrition is very important.

Milk is the child's first food. It has a large amount of the nutrients needed during the first two years of life. The kind of milk or formula must be chosen with care.

Human milk is custom-made for the baby. It is clean and pure. It saves a lot of work. Nursing can also be a satisfying experience for both mother and baby. Human milk will usually supply enough of all the important nutrients during the first few months of life, except for vitamin D, fluoride and iron.

If a prepared formula, evaporated milk or homogenized whole milk is used, it will usually have vitamin D added to it. If not, the baby will need to be given vitamin D in addition to its regular milk.

The baby needs vitamin C early in life. Human milk and prepared formulas usually have good amounts of vitamin C. If the baby is being fed evaporated milk or cow's milk formula, then vitamin C should be given in the form of drops. Otherwise a fresh, frozen or canned fruit juice that is naturally rich in vitamin C can be used.

A source of iron should also be added to the child's diet. Some formulas already have iron added. If the baby is getting a formula that does not have iron, then the doctor may start the baby on iron drops. This is mostly done when the child is about one or two months old.

Solid foods may be added when the child is one to three months old. Slowly, other foods, such as egg yolk, strained meat and fish, are added. Be careful when choosing baby's food. Store-bought strained foods vary widely. They vary in the amount of calories and other nutrients they contain. This is why many mothers decide to prepare their own baby food at home. At least they know what their babies are getting.

By the time baby is six months old, he or she will be taking some "table food." When seven to nine months old, a baby is usually ready for foods that are chopped. By then, he or she will likely be on three meals a day.

Choose the foods for your baby carefully. Your baby will be happier and healthier if you do.

Selection 17: Recalling Facts

1. A child's first food is
   □ a. juice.   □ b. milk.   □ c. water.

2. Human milk does not supply enough vitamin D, fluoride and
   □ a. iron.   □ b. salt.   □ c. sugar.

3. A prepared formula contains good amounts of
   □ a. fat.   □ b. starch.   □ c. vitamin C.

4. A doctor may give a baby iron drops when the child is one or two
   □ a. hours old.   □ b. days old.   □ c. months old.

5. A nine-month-old child is ready for foods that are
   □ a. chopped.   □ b. spicy.   □ c. fried.

Selection 17: Understanding Ideas

6. Choose the best title for this article.
   □ a. Baby's First Foods
   □ b. The Importance of Iron
   □ c. Learning to Walk

7. What is the main idea of this article?
   □ a. Good nutrition is important for an infant.
   □ b. Many infants eat too much.
   □ c. Vitamin D is the most important vitamin.

8. Vitamin C can be found in most
   □ a. fruit juices.   □ b. red meats.   □ c. starchy foods.

9. Strained meat is added to a baby's diet
   □ a. all at once.   □ b. gradually.   □ c. not at all.

10. A child starts eating three meals a day when it is about
    □ a. one month old.
    □ b. nine months old.
    □ c. twenty-four months old.

18. For Today, Tomorrow and Always

Almost all foods give us energy. Some give us more energy than others. Energy is measured in calories. Foods rich in fats, starches or sugars have a lot of calories. Fat is a big source of energy.

At times you eat foods that have more energy, or calories, than you need. The extra energy is then stored in the body as fat. If you eat too much, you become overweight. When you eat fewer calories than the body uses, you lose weight.

The body can pick and choose what it needs from the nutrients in the diet. Your body sees to it that each organ gets exactly the right amount of nutrients it needs. However, if the diet lacks some of the needed nutrients, the body has no way of getting them.

Your body keeps busy. It works twenty-four hours a day. It is always building itself up, repairing itself, and getting rid of waste products. It needs a constant supply of nutrients to do its job. When it receives the nutrients, it sends them where they are needed.

Let's take calcium as an example. The body needs calcium. Calcium helps to clot blood. It also helps build bones. Calcium helps make the nerves and muscles work well. If your body does not get enough calcium from the food you eat, it steals some from your bones. If the stolen calcium is not replaced, the body is in trouble. You may not realize this fact for some years. As much as one-third of the normal amount of calcium may be taken from an adult's bones before the loss shows up on an X-ray film.

Nutrients working with other nutrients make the difference in our health and well-being. No single nutrient can work properly alone. For example, it takes calcium to build strong bones, but that is only the beginning. Without vitamin D, the calcium cannot be taken into the body. The use of protein is another example. Protein forms part of every cell and all the fluids tha travel in and around the cells. However, it takes vitamin C to help make the fluids between the cells. Without vitamin C, the protein could not do its job.

The foods you eat keep you healthy for today, but they also build your body for a lifetime. They keep you well today, tomorrow and always.

Selection 18: Recalling Facts

1. Energy is measured in
   ☐ a. calories.   ☐ b. pounds.   ☐ c. watts.

2. Which of these is a big source of energy?
   ☐ a. Fats   ☐ b. Vegetables   ☐ c. Water

3. If you eat too much, you become
   ☐ a. active.   ☐ b. graceful.   ☐ c. overweight.

4. Calcium helps to build
   ☐ a. bones.   ☐ b. muscles.   ☐ c. tissues.

5. Protein forms part of every
   ☐ a. cell.   ☐ b. nutrient.   ☐ c. vitamin.

Selection 18: Understanding Ideas

6. Our energy comes from the
   ☐ a. clothes we wear.
   ☐ b. foods we eat.
   ☐ c. water we drink.

7. This article hints that, in order to work properly, your body needs
   ☐ a. electricity.
   ☐ b. nutrients.
   ☐ c. tobacco.

8. We can see that our blood contains a good amount of
   ☐ a. calcium.   ☐ b. fat.   ☐ c. X-rays.

9. Without calcium, our bones would become very
   ☐ a. damp.   ☐ b. strong.   ☐ c. weak.

10. What is the main idea of this article?
    ☐ a. The foods we eat keep us healthy.
    ☐ b. Our bodies need daily exercise.
    ☐ c. Protein is not always good for us.

19. A Pressing Choice

Reading Time _____

Comprehension Score _____

Words per Minute _____

Modern electric irons have made ironing and pressing clothes an easy job. But there are a few things you should know about different kinds of irons. Then you can choose the iron that best suits your needs.

The dry iron is simple. It is cheap. Its only working parts are a heating element, a thermostat and a temperature setting. It is mainly used on heavy, dampened cloth. On the other hand, steam and steam/spray irons are used for many different jobs.

The steam/spray iron has a nozzle that sprays water to help remove wrinkles. With the steam on, it can touch up permanent press clothes. It can raise the nap on velvets and corduroys. And it can block knits or press wools. With the steam off, it can be used as dry irons.

The dry iron and the steam and steam/spray irons are rather bulky. However, the travel iron is small and light. It has a handle that folds. It can be easily packed into a suitcase. Some travel irons also have steam or steam/spray features.

After you decide upon the type of iron you want, there are other things you should check. The controls on an iron should be well marked and easy to work. Grasp the handle of the iron you like. Hold it in the ironing position. If you must shift your grasp to see or use the controls, the iron will be difficult to use. Try another brand or style.

The heel rest, which may be the broad back of the handle or a handle with crosspieces, should be strong. The iron should not tip easily when in the rest, or upright, position. As a test, place the iron upright. Next, push gently against the top. If the iron falls easily then you might want to choose another.

One more thing to look at is the electrical cord on the iron. Check to make sure that the cord is well placed. The cord should be placed so you can iron with either hand on either side of the ironing board. Some irons have cords that can be moved from one side of the handle to the other. On other irons the cords cannot be moved. You must decide which is best for you. Choose your iron with care, and you will be well satisfied with your choice.

Selection 19: Recalling Facts

1. How many working parts does the dry iron have?
    ☐ a. One   ☐ b. Two   ☐ c. Three

2. The dry iron is mostly used on
    ☐ a. fine, silk cloth.
    ☐ b. heavy, dampened cloth.
    ☐ c. permanent press cloth.

3. Steam irons can raise the nap on
    ☐ a. cotton.   ☐ b. silk.   ☐ c. velvet.

4. A steam/spray iron has a special nozzle that sprays
    ☐ a. bleach.   ☐ b. starch.   ☐ c. water.

5. The travel iron is small and
    ☐ a. bulky.   ☐ b. colorful.   ☐ c. light.

Selection 19: Understanding Ideas

6. Electric irons make ironing
    ☐ a. difficult.   ☐ b. easy.   ☐ c. hard.

7. This article hints that
    ☐ a. ironing clothes is a woman's job.
    ☐ b. some people do not like to iron.
    ☐ c. there are different kinds of irons.

8. Steam irons can also be used as
    ☐ a. branding irons.   ☐ b. dry irons.   ☐ c. flat irons.

9. You can remove wrinkles from cloth by
    ☐ a. folding it in a towel.
    ☐ b. washing it in bleach and water.
    ☐ c. wetting and then ironing it.

10. A good heel rest is
    ☐ a. firm.   ☐ b. pretty.   ☐ c. unsteady.

20. Minerals Make the Difference

Reading Time _____

Comprehension Score _____

Words per Minute _____

Minerals are needed for a healthy body. They are needed to help our bodies grow. The most plentiful mineral in the body is calcium. Yet, it may not be found in many diets. Studies show that a lack of calcium may be found in all age groups. For instance, from the age of nine, the diets of girls and women may not have enough calcium. Their diets may lack as much as 25 to 30 percent of the calcium they need.

Almost all calcium is in bones and teeth. The rest is found in the tissue and body fluids. Calcium is needed for blood to clot. It is also needed for the heart to work properly. The nervous system does not work well when calcium levels in the blood are low. Even muscles work better when the body gets enough calcium.

Most people who buy from the milk counter are stocking up on calcium supplies. In the U.S. we depend on milk as a big source of calcium. Two cups of milk, or an equal amount of cheese or other dairy products, gives us a lot of calcium. They go a long way toward giving us all the calcium needed for the day.

But milk is not the only source of calcium. Dark green leafy vegetables like collards, mustard greens or turnip greens have some calcium. Salmon and sardines give us useful amounts of it if the very tiny bones are eaten.

Calcium is not the only important mineral in the body. Iron is important, too. Women of child-bearing age need more iron than men. The diets of infants and pregnant women may need to be watched closely to see that they have the iron they should.

Only a few foods have iron in large amounts. Liver, heart, kidney and lean meats have a good deal of it. Shellfish, especially oysters, have a lot of iron. Whole grain and enriched breads and cereals are rich in iron. They give us up to one quarter of the daily iron we need. Dark green leafy vegetables are also sources of iron.

Calcium and iron are not the only minerals you need. Most of the other minerals your body needs are found in so many foods that a little variety in making your choice at the market can easily take care of them. Make a healthy, happy body your goal next time you food shop.

Selection 20: Recalling Facts

1. Calcium is a
   □ a. fat. □ b. mineral. □ c. vitamin.

2. Almost all calcium is found in the bones and
   □ a. hair. □ b. nails. □ c. teeth.

3. Calcium is needed
   □ a. to carry waste. □ b. to clot blood. □ c. to fight infection.

4. A big source of calcium is
   □ a. fat. □ b. milk. □ c. water.

5. Which of the following vegetables contains calcium?
   □ a. Collards □ b. Potatoes □ c. Squash

Selection 20: Understanding Ideas

6. What two minerals does this article talk about?
   □ a. Calcium and iron
   □ b. Iodine and calcium
   □ c. Potassium and sodium

7. What is the main idea of this article?
   □ a. The body needs minerals in order to stay healthy.
   □ b. Vegetables contain very few vitamins and minerals.
   □ c. Vitamins are more important for a healthy body than minerals.

8. This article hints that many people
   □ a. do not like foods that contain calcium.
   □ b. lack enough calcium in their daily diets.
   □ c. over-cook their dark green leafy vegetables.

9. We can see that
   □ a. infants need more iron than adult men.
   □ b. pregnant women need very little iron.
   □ c. women do not need as much iron as men.

10. Oysters are a type of
   □ a. mammal. □ b. reptile. □ c. shellfish.

21. Look Around You

Reading Time _____

Comprehension Score _____

Words per Minute _____

The environment is everything about you. It can be living, like a forest. It can be non-living, like a rock mountain. An environment can be natural or man-made.

There are many kinds of environments. There are cities, small towns and farms. There are oceans, lakes, deserts and forests. Each of these has its own mixture of living things and non-living things. Even man-made environments, such as cities, have both living and non-living things. An environment may have such living things as birds, fish and plants. It has such non-living things as air, soil and water.

Many animals and plants are found in only one kind of environment. Man, however, can be found in almost all environments. He can even visit places where he needs special things to live, such as the moon.

No living thing can live alone. Every living thing depends upon other things in its environment. When something changes, it has an effect on something else. If a non-living thing like water becomes hard to find, plants will be affected. If plants die out, the animals who eat plants will be affected.

Weather, such as temperature, wind and rain, can change an environment. People can change an environment, too. Some things that people do cause no change or only a small change in the environment. For instance, people can walk through the woods and just look. People can cut down only a few trees from a large area and still not change the environment very much.

On the other hand, some things that people do cause a lot of change. They can change a whole environment by cutting down a forest.

Not all changes are bad. If we cut down a forest to build houses, plant crops or make paper, this may not be bad. But what if we cut down all trees in all forests to do these things? What if we didn't save some and replace others? What effect would this have on other living and non-living things in our environment?

It is clear that people have the power to change an environment. What they do has an affect on all the living and non-living things there. This is why it is important to think about the changes before we make them. When people make wise choices, the environment stays healthy. Let's all work together to keep it clean and healthy.

Selection 21: Recalling Facts

1. Which of the following is non-living?
   □ a. Air   □ b. Fish   □ c. Plants

2. Which environment is man-made?
   □ a. Cities   □ b. Deserts   □ c. Forests

3. If water becomes hard to find, which of the following is most affected?
   □ a. Buildings   □ b. Plants   □ c. Rocks

4. A whole environment can be changed by
   □ a. cutting down a forest.
   □ b. painting a country scene.
   □ c. walking through the woods.

5. Before we change anything in an environment, we should
   □ a. ignore any changes.
   □ b. kill all living things.
   □ c. think about the changes.

Selection 21: Understanding Ideas

6. Choose the best title for this article.
   □ a. The Environment and You
   □ b. Pollution Is Everywhere
   □ c. Water and Air to Clean

7. This article hints that man
   □ a. can travel from one environment to another.
   □ b. does not enjoy living on the planet Earth.
   □ c. ignores the non-living environments around us.

8. Man cannot live on the moon unless he has special
   □ a. equipment..   □ b. friends.   □ c. weapons.

9. We can see that an environment can easily be destroyed by
   □ a. disease.   □ b. man.   □ c. nature.

10. In order to save the environment for our future needs, we must
    □ a. destroy all non-living things.
    □ b. keep our environment healthy.
    □ c. kill all animals of prey.

22. Think about It

Reading Time _____

Comprehension Score _____

Words per Minute _____

Escaping a fire is a serious matter. Knowing what to do before a fire breaks out can save a life. For example, people should know the safety measures to take before opening a hall door during a fire. Also, make sure everyone knows how to unlock doors that may be in the escape path. At times, a key is needed to unlock a door from the inside. So, keep the key in the lock. Or, you can put the key on a key-ring and put it where it can be found easily.

If you live in an apartment, know the ways you can use to get out. Show everyone in the family these ways. Stress the importance of using stairways or fire escapes, not elevators.

From most homes and the lower floors of apartment buildings, escape through windows is possible. Learn the best way of leaving by a window with the least chance of serious injury.

In a home fire, windows are often the only way to escape. The second floor window sill is usually not more than 13 feet from the ground. An average person, hanging by the fingertips, will have a drop of about six feet to the ground. Often, a second floor window opens onto a porch roof or balcony. From there, it is possible to drop to the ground or await rescue.

Windows are also useful when you're waiting for help. Often you'll be able to stay in the room for several minutes if you keep the door closed and the window open. Keep your head low in the window to be sure you get fresh air rather than smoke that may have leaked into the room.

On a second or third floor, the best windows for escape are those which open onto a roof or balcony. From the roof or balcony, a person can either drop to the ground or await rescue. Dropping onto cement walks or pavement might end in injury. Bushes, soft earth and grass can help to break a fall. A rope ladder should be considered when the drop is too great.

In a town where the fire department acts quickly, it may be best to wait for rescue. Close the doors and wait by an open window for help. Shout for help. Be sure to close the door before opening a window. Otherwise, smoke and fire may be drawn into the room by the draft.

57

Selection 22: Recalling Facts

1. Which of the following should not be used when trying to escape a fire?
   ☐ a. Elevators　　　　☐ b. Fire escapes　　　　☐ c. Stairways

2. From most homes you can escape a fire through the
   ☐ a. attic.　　　　☐ b. garage.　　　　☐ c. windows.

3. How far from the ground is the second floor window sill?
   ☐ a. 13 feet　　　　☐ b. 25 feet　　　　☐ c. 32 feet

4. Often, a second floor window opens onto a porch roof or
   ☐ a. balcony.　　　　☐ b. driveway.　　　　☐ c. patio.

5. Which of the following helps to break a fall from a second floor window?
   ☐ a. Cement　　　　☐ b. Grass　　　　☐ c. Pavement

Selection 22: Understanding Ideas

6. This article tells us how
   ☐ a. to escape a fire.　　☐ b. to put out a fire.　　☐ c. to start a fire.

7. This article hints that windows are
   ☐ a. easily broken.
   ☐ b. good escape routes.
   ☐ c. often hard to open.

8. If you are trapped in a room during a fire, it's a good idea
   ☐ a. to lie under the bed.
   ☐ b. to open a window.
   ☐ c. to stand perfectly still.

9. We can see from this article that
   ☐ a. breathing in smoke might be harmful.
   ☐ b. rope ladders should not be used in a fire.
   ☐ c. youngsters often start most home fires.

10. What is the main idea of this article?
    ☐ a. Firemen are not well paid or well trained.
    ☐ b. It is not a good idea to smoke in bed or on a couch.
    ☐ c. People should know what to do before a fire breaks out.

23. Exploring the Unknown

Reading Time _____

Comprehension Score _____

Words per Minute _____

The Kennedy Space Center is busy once again. The Florida spaceport had been quiet for about three years. Before then it had been the launch site for the moon flights and manned missions. Now it is getting ready for a new chapter of space history.

The new age of space flight will start with the first flight of NASA's Space Shuttle. The shuttle has a system that can be reused. This will greatly reduce costs. The shuttle will also make it easier for man to reach outer space. It will give NASA a new tool to help man explore space.

The new shuttle will be rocket-launched like all spacecraft. But there is now a difference. Its two boosters can be recovered and reused. Also, the manned part of the shuttle acts like a piloted craft in space. It will return to earth, landing like an airplane.

We can see that space travel will no longer need highly trained astronauts. Along with its crew of three, the shuttle will hold up to four scientists. All of them can work without having to wear any special spacesuits. They can test and study the heavens from space. They will be able to send back to earth reports about weather and other conditions that can be seen from the craft. Remember, they will have a bird's-eye view of earth.

The shuttle will allow the inspace repair of other spacecraft. It will also be able to bring spacecraft back to earth for work that cannot be done in space.

Some space jobs were once impossible or too expensive. But now with the help of the shuttle they can be done. The shuttle opens the door to some new ideas. Space cities can now be built. The building blocks for such cities will be delivered by the shuttle. Many power space stations will be built, too. These stations will be able to turn the sun's energy into electricity that can be used back on Earth.

Economy is the key to the shuttle. Since it can be reused, costly one-shot launchings can be a thing of the past. Satellites already in space can be kept there longer. Their lifespans will be longer because they can now be easily repaired. The shuttle will not need the expensive sea recovery that was used during past space flights. The savings to the space program could well be over a billion dollars a year!

Selection 23: Recalling Facts

1. The Kennedy Space Center is in
    □ a. Florida.   □ b. Iowa.   □ c. Texas.

2. How long has the Kennedy Space Center been quiet?
    □ a. One year   □ b. Two years   □ c. Three years

3. The Space Shuttle will greatly reduce costs because it can be
    □ a. destroyed.   □ b. reused.   □ c. stored.

4. How many crew members will be used on the shuttle?
    □ a. One   □ b. Two   □ c. Three

5. In the future, power space stations will be able to turn the sun's energy into
    □ a. electricity.   □ b. gas.   □ c. oil.

Selection 23: Understanding Ideas

6. Up until the time of the Space Shuttle, moon flights and manned space missions were
    □ a. dangerous.   □ b. expensive.   □ c. impossible.

7. NASA seems to deal mostly with
    □ a. exploring space.
    □ b. measuring earthquakes.
    □ c. studying ocean life.

8. All spacecraft are launched by
    □ a. stations.   □ b. towers.   □ c. rockets.

9. The Space Shuttle can hold at least
    □ a. seven people.   □ b. twenty people.   □ c. fifty people.

10. The Space Shuttle will make space travel
    □ a. easier.   □ b. harder.   □ c. harmful.

24. A Gallon Saved

There are more than 100 million cars in the United States. A typical car gets less than 15 miles from each gallon of gas. It travels about 10,000 miles each year. In that time, it uses about 650 gallons of gas. In all, autos use up some 70 billion gallons of gas a year. That comes out to be four-and-a-half million barrels a day.

The importance of saving gas, then, cannot be stressed too much. Let's say, for instance, that the fuel used by each car could be cut back just 15 percent. This could be done by making fewer trips each day. It could be done by keeping autos in better shape. It could be done through better driving habits. If it were done, our nation's use of fuel would fall by nearly two-thirds of a million barrels per day.

We can all help to save gas. One way is to ride the buses, or to walk to work. We could ride mopeds or bicycles. Another way is to share a ride. We could join car-pools. About one-third of all private cars are used for going to and from work.

Go shopping with a neighbor from time to time. If two people use a car instead of one, everyone saves. Driving stress would be less, too, with fewer cars on the road. The savings on gas around the nation would come to more than one-half million barrels a day.

Another way to save is by cutting out useless trips. Can you find one driving trip per week that could be handled by telephone? Can you combine trips? If each car took one less 10-mile trip a week, we could save three-and-a-half billion gallons of gas a year. This comes to nearly 5 percent of the total passenger car demand for gas.

The way people drive decides how much fuel they save. Careful drivers may get 20 percent more miles per gallon than normal drivers. They could get 50 percent more miles per gallon than wasteful drivers. Careful drivers obey the 55-mile-per-hour speed limit. They get to their desired speed quickly and keep a steady pace.

If just one gallon of gas were saved each week for each auto in the country, we could all save about five-and-a-half billion gallons a year.

Selection 24: Recalling Facts

1. There are more than 100 million cars in
   ☐ a. Canada.   ☐ b. Europe.   ☐ c. the U.S.

2. An average car travels 10,000 miles each
   ☐ a. week.   ☐ b. month.   ☐ c. year.

3. Keeping your car in good shape helps you save
   ☐ a. coal.   ☐ b. gas.   ☐ c. water.

4. About one-third of all private cars are used for going to and from
   ☐ a. school.   ☐ b. vacations.   ☐ c. work.

5. To do away with useless car trips, you can use the
   ☐ a. dictionary.   ☐ b. library.   ☐ c. telephone.

Selection 24: Understanding Ideas

6. What is the main idea of this article?
   ☐ a. Americans need to save gas.
   ☐ b. Gas prices continue to rise.
   ☐ c. Small cars get good gas mileage.

7. A typical car gets 15 miles to the gallon. This figure is
   ☐ a. an average.   ☐ b. a guess.   ☐ c. a minimum.

8. Sharing a ride with a friend is called
   ☐ a. carloading.   ☐ b. carpooling.   ☐ c. cartraveling.

9. If more people shared a ride, there would be
   ☐ a. fewer cars on the road.
   ☐ b. higher insurance rates.
   ☐ c. more highway accidents.

10. This article hints that a careful driver travels about
    ☐ a. 55 miles per hour.
    ☐ b. 65 miles per hour.
    ☐ c. 75 miles per hour.

25. Busy Little Creatures

Reading Time _____

Comprehension Score _____

Words per Minute _____

Most homeowners know that termites can hurt the wood in their homes. Over the years, these insects have caused great damage over much of the United States. If termites are found in the home, there is no cause for panic. They can be controlled.

Underground termites live in large groups called colonies. The workers and soldiers spend their entire lives underground or completely buried in wood. Thus, they are rarely seen. Termites need high humidity in order to live. They keep their nests humid by using moisture from the soil. But, sometimes there is enough moisture in the wood itself. Because underground termites do not like dry air, they remain buried. So, the damage they cause goes unnoticed.

Winged termites inside a house are almost a sure sign of trouble. They are easy to spot. They have yellow-brown to black bodies. Their two pairs of wings are of equal size. Winged ants have two pairs of unequal sized wings. Also, termites have thick waistlines; ants have hourglass figures.

Once they nest, the termites shed their wings. Wings are often found beneath doors or windows. Because the winged termites are drawn to light, their wings may be found around light fixtures. If you find wings inside the house, you can guess that termites have moved in.

Damage to wood cannot be seen unless the outside of the wood is stripped away. When it is, many paths are found in the wood. Workers may usually be seen when a piece of damaged wood is studied. Both the workers and soldiers are wingless and grayish white in color. The workers feed on the wood while the soldiers guard the colony. The two forms look alike, but the soldiers have larger heads and jaws.

The only sure way to stop termite attacks or to get rid of them is to cut off their source of moisture. Without moisture, a colony will die. Keep in mind that termites can attack dry wood. They can do this by bringing in their own moisture from the soil.

In some places termites are common. Homeowners can make sure they are safe from attack by calling a pest control company. This kind of company first checks the house. It then does whatever is needed to kill the termites. The cost of this treatment depends on the amount of work to be done. But it is better to be safe than sorry.

Selection 25: Recalling Facts

1. Underground termites live in large groups called
   □ a. colonies.   □ b. cities.   □ c. gangs.

2. Sometimes worker and soldier termites spend their whole lives buried in
   □ a. clay.   □ b. rock.   □ c. wood.

3. Termites get the moisture they need from
   □ a. nearby ponds.   □ b. the soil.   □ c. wells.

4. Winged termites are either yellow-brown or
   □ a. black.   □ b. orange.   □ c. white.

5. What color are the worker and soldier termites?
   □ a. Brownish black   □ b. Grayish white   □ c. Yellow-black

Selection 25: Understanding Ideas

6. Termites are a type of
   □ a. fungus.   □ b. insect.   □ c. mineral.

7. In order to live, termites need
   □ a. sunlight.   □ b. sugar.   □ c. water.

8. Some termites are hard to spot because
   □ a. they only come out at night.
   □ b. they live underground.
   □ c. they travel very fast.

9. We can see from this article that some termites can
   □ a. fly.   □ b. hop.   □ c. jump.

10. Termites and ants
    □ a. have different body shapes.
    □ b. live side by side.
    □ c. often attack and kill each other.

26. A Measure in Metrics

What do metric measures mean to you? They should mean a lot. In 1972 Congress talked about changing from the English system of measure to the metric. Some countries have already made the switch. As the use of metric measures increases, you will see a change in your nearby food store. You will see metric units used for weight, volume and length.

Right now, the number of different units you meet in a day's shopping is puzzling. Weights are shown in ounces and pounds. Liquids are measured in gallons, quarts, pints and fluid ounces. Dry measures are shown in bushels, pecks, dry quarts and pints. However, all of that will be made easier under the metric system. With metric units, weight will be shown only in grams or kilograms. Volume will be shown only in liters or kiloliters. Length will be measured in meters, centimeters or millimeters only. Clearly, metric is much less confusing and will be much easier to use when shopping than the English system.

Some of the most common measurements made in the home are those that take place in cooking and baking. The practice that will be most often followed in metric recipes should not differ from our current practice. Metric "cup and spoon" measures are only slightly larger than the cup and spoon measures we are used to. They can be interchanged. It is only those few ingredients that are now measured by weight (pounds and ounces) that will change a lot in the metric system. To change a recipe to metric, just remember that a pound is about 450 grams and an ounce is about 28 grams.

Sales people in hardware, paint and fabric stores will feel the change to metric. A customer may want to buy lumber or paint or wallpaper. He may give the clerk his measurements in English units. The clerk in turn will have to change the units to metric. At least figuring in metric is not at all difficult. Again, it is easier to use then the English system.

The change over to metric is coming. It should not scare you. It is an easy and simple system to use. For most people, the knowledge of metric units that they learn as customers will help them. Slowly they will get used to using the new system. Who knows, maybe some day the English system will be completely forgotten.

65

Selection 26: Recalling Facts

1. Weights can be shown in ounces and
   - ☐ a. feet.
   - ☐ b. inches.
   - ☐ c. pounds.

2. Fluids are measured in
   - ☐ a. gallons.
   - ☐ b. pounds.
   - ☐ c. yards.

3. In metric labeling, weight will be shown only in grams or
   - ☐ a. kilograms.
   - ☐ b. kiloliters.
   - ☐ c. kilowatts.

4. Using the metric system, length will be measured in meters, centimeters or
   - ☐ a. dekagrams.
   - ☐ b. kiloliters.
   - ☐ c. millimeters.

5. A pound is about
   - ☐ a. 100 grams.
   - ☐ b. 250 grams.
   - ☐ c. 450 grams.

Selection 26: Understanding Ideas

6. The metric system is used in
   - ☐ a. card shops.
   - ☐ b. grocery stores.
   - ☐ c. pet stores.

7. The metric system is
   - ☐ a. confusing to use.
   - ☐ b. easy to use.
   - ☐ c. hard to use.

8. This article hints that cooking and baking require a lot of
   - ☐ a. measuring.
   - ☐ b. preparing.
   - ☐ c. sampling.

9. We can see that sales people will need
   - ☐ a. to know their customers.
   - ☐ b. to learn the metric system.
   - ☐ c. to travel a lot.

10. We can see that
    - ☐ a. cloth is often measured by the size of the bolt.
    - ☐ b. metric units are confusing and silly.
    - ☐ c. some people might be afraid to use the metric system.

27. Probing with a Purpose

NASA's space science program is yielding a wealth of knowledge. In the summer of 1977, NASA launched two Voyager probes. They are now on their endless journey into space. On their way, the probes will explore the planets. The probes will pass Jupiter, Saturn and maybe Uranus. The crafts will then whirl through space. They may travel for millions of years.

The Voyager program is a big help to NASA. It gives NASA a close look at the planets. From the Voyager's flight, new facts can be gathered. The questions of the beginnings and workings of the solar system may now soon be answered.

Studying the planets is only one part of a carefully planned space science program. NASA is also studying Earth, its moon and its atmosphere. Studying our sun and the stars of our galaxy are other goals of the program. In life research, we hope to gain knowledge of the effect that space has on living things. The well-known tools of this great project are the deep-space probes and the satellites. Less well known is the use of rockets, special aircraft and even balloons. Such things like radio telescopes are also used in the study.

The purpose behind this probing and searching is the same as that of all research— to help mankind. In space science, the benefits may not be seen right away. Still, they are valuable to the future of us all.

Today's scientists may not be able to find a use for some of the knowledge gained in the space science program. Still, what we learn today may be useful tomorrow. As we learn more and more about our world, pieces of the puzzle begin to fit together. Scientists of tomorrow may find uses for this knowledge that will benefit future generations.

All of the goals of NASA's space science program share a common end. They all want to learn more about Earth. Only by exploring other bodies in the skies can we answer some of the questions we have about Earth. The things we have learned about other planets have helped us to know our own planet better. It is important to understand the forces that control Earth. With that understanding we may be able to manage those forces. This control would help mankind. It will help improve our lives. It will give our children a better world in which to live.

Selection 27: Recalling Facts

1. NASA's space science program is giving us a lot of
    □ a. knowledge.   □ b. talent.   □ c. trouble.

2. In what year were the Voyager probes launched?
    □ a. 1975   □ b. 1976   □ c. 1977

3. Which of the following planets will the Voyagers pass?
    □ a. Jupiter   □ b. Neptune   □ c. Pluto

4. NASA is also interested in the Earth's moon and its
    □ a. atmosphere.   □ b. mountains.   □ c. oceans.

5. In order to gain information about the planets, NASA uses deep-space probes and
    □ a. comets.   □ b. meteors.   □ c. satellites.

Selection 27: Understanding Ideas

6. Which of these would be a good title for the article?
    □ a. How to Build a Spaceship
    □ b. NASA's Space Science Program
    □ c. Visitors from Outer Space

7. After the probes pass Jupiter, Saturn and Uranus, they will probably
    □ a. burn up.
    □ b. keep on going.
    □ c. return to Earth.

8. The Voyager program gives us knowledge of other
    □ a. people.   □ b. planets.   □ c. religions.

9. The goal of all research is
    □ a. to destroy life on other planets.
    □ b. to make things better for man.
    □ c. to stop war before it starts.

10. This article hints that some knowledge cannot be used right away, so it is
    □ a. completely forgotten.
    □ b. kept for later use.
    □ c. ignored and destroyed.

28. A Useful Gun Indeed

Reading Time _____

Comprehension Score _____

Words per Minute _____

Paint sprayers are very useful for large surfaces. A spray gun is faster than a brush or a roller. Some paint may be wasted through over-spraying. Even so, the time and effort you save more than make up for the extra paint. It takes a little time at first to learn how to spray. Once you have learned, it takes no time at all to produce a thick and even coat of paint.

Spraying is a good way to cover surfaces that are rough and uneven. Things that are hard to paint with a brush or roller are quickly done with a sprayer. A spray gun can be used for any coat except the prime coat. The surface to be sprayed must be clean and free of dust. Paint that is sprayed will not stick if a film of dust is present.

When you use a sprayer, special care must be taken to prepare the paint. Stir or strain the paint to remove any lumps. Thin the paint carefully. Be sure there aren't any lumps and the paint is not too thick. Thick paint will clog the gun. Thin paint will sag and run after it is sprayed. Follow the instructions on the can. Use the type and amount of thinner that is shown.

Before you begin, ask your paint dealer to show you how the sprayer works. He will be able to give you some useful pointers. Adjust the gun so that the width of the spray is the same size as the surface to be covered. A narrow spray is best for small surfaces. A wide spray should be used for things like walls or table tops.

Hold the spray gun about eight inches from the surface to be painted. Start to spray while the gun is slightly beyond the surface. This assures a smooth, even flow when you reach the area to be coated. Move the sprayer parallel to the surface. Move the sprayer evenly back and forth across the area. Spray the corners and edges first.

Cover everything close to the work with drop cloths or newspapers. The "bounce-back" from the sprayer may spread several feet from the work surface. Be careful not to breathe in the paint dust. Use a mask if needed. When spraying, the tip of the spray gun may become clogged. Use a broom straw to clean it. Never use wire or a nail.

Selection 28: Recalling Facts

1. Paint sprayers are used to paint
    - ☐ a. narrow trims.
    - ☐ b. large surfaces.
    - ☐ c. small areas.

2. Before you spray a surface, it must be free of
    - ☐ a. dust.
    - ☐ b. paint.
    - ☐ c. scratches.

3. How far away from the surface to be painted should you hold the spray gun?
    - ☐ a. Two inches
    - ☐ b. Four inches
    - ☐ c. Eight inches

4. A narrow spray is best for
    - ☐ a. rough surfaces.
    - ☐ b. uneven surfaces.
    - ☐ c. small surfaces.

5. If the tip of the spray gun becomes clogged, you can clean it with a
    - ☐ a. broom straw.
    - ☐ b. thin wire.
    - ☐ c. thick nail.

Selection 28: Understanding Ideas

6. A paint sprayer
    - ☐ a. is hard to use.
    - ☐ b. makes painting easier.
    - ☐ c. uses very little paint.

7. It seems that paint sprayers
    - ☐ a. do not do a good job on rough surfaces.
    - ☐ b. can be used to paint small surfaces.
    - ☐ c. use more paint than paint brushes do.

8. Spray paint will not stick to a
    - ☐ a. clean surface.
    - ☐ b. dirty surface.
    - ☐ c. rough surface.

9. We can see that lumpy paint
    - ☐ a. keeps the paint sprayer working well.
    - ☐ b. makes the paint sprayer work better.
    - ☐ c. will eventually harm a paint sprayer.

10. This article hints that paint sprayers
    - ☐ a. are expensive to buy.
    - ☐ b. give off a fine paint dust.
    - ☐ c. use extra-thick paint.

29. A Pest Problem

Reading Time _____

Comprehension Score _____

Words per Minute _____

Pesticides are chemicals that kill. They can reduce or stop the growth of pests. Pests include insects, fish, rats, mice, fungi, weeds and other harmful animals or plants. Pests are bad because they spoil food. They spoil clothing, household furnishings and buildings. They injure, kill and spread disease to people. Pests can also harm helpful animals and plants.

Helpful animals and plants are those that people like and make use of. Or they are ones that are important to a healthy world. These include living things that give us food, such as crops and cattle. It also includes plants used as decoration and cats and dogs kept as pets. Also in this group are the animals and plants found in nature that people enjoy or ones that are needed to keep a smooth and even balance. So, to protect plants and animals from harm, we use pesticides.

Pesticides are helpful. However, they can be harmful, too. Pesticides can be misused. They can be used without following the right directions. When this happens, they do a great amount of harm to the very animals and plants that we want to protect. Pesticides can poison. The deadly effects of these poisons can last a long time. The remains of some pesticides last for many years. They harm and kill long after they were first used.

The message is clear. Pesticides are useful. They protect us and our useful plants and animals. But if not used in the right way, pesticides can harm us and the animals and plants we want to protect. You can never be too careful when using pesticides.

Guard yourself and others from pesticides. It is not safe for children to use pesticides. In some cases, it is against the law for youngsters to use pesticides. Pest control is a job for grown ups.

Teach your child well. Children should be able to know a pesticide by the label on the package. They should be taught not to touch or use empty pesticide jars or cans. Spilled pesticides on the outside of the package can be unsafe. They can poison someone.

Sometimes people are poisoned by a pesticide. If this happens, follow the directions on the label which tell you what to do.

Ways to control pests without using pesticides need to be found and tested. Perhaps someday in the future we will learn to control pests without using pesticides.

Selection 29: Recalling Facts

1. Pesticides are
   □ a. chemicals.   □ b. minerals.   □ c. vitamins.

2. Pests spoil
   □ a. food.   □ b. paint.   □ c. oil.

3. Which of the following are useful animals?
   □ a. Cattle   □ b. Mice   □ c. Rats

4. Pesticides should never be used by
   □ a. adults.   □ b. children.   □ c. people.

5. If someone is poisoned by a pesticide, you should follow the directions on the
   □ a. handle.   □ b. label.   □ c. lid.

Selection 29: Understanding Ideas

6. What is the main idea of this article?
   □ a. Harmful pests do much damage to clothing.
   □ b. Pesticides can be helpful as well as harmful.
   □ c. Useful animals often carry many diseases.

7. Some people like to decorate their houses with
   □ a. pests.   □ b. plants.   □ c. poison.

8. This article hints that pesticides are
   □ a. easy to use.
   □ b. expensive to buy.
   □ c. harmful to children.

9. Often pesticides are dangerous because they
   □ a. are not used properly.
   □ b. are stored in the garage.
   □ c. explode easily.

10. New ways to control pests
    □ a. are being tested.
    □ b. are easily found.
    □ c. are not needed.

30. Do-It-Yourself

Reading Time _____

Comprehension Score _____

Words per Minute _____

Many kinds of insulation can be used for the home. Kinds that are easily installed make good do-it-yourself tasks. These kinds include batts, blankets and loose fill. Avoid plastic foam. It is best installed by a contractor who has special tools for the job.

Batts and blankets are made of glass fiber or rock wool. Batts come in packs of four-foot lengths or eight-foot lengths. Blankets come in rolls. Both are sold in widths of 15 or 23 inches to fit normal spaces in house frames. Both come in thicknesses of 1 to 7 inches. Both batts and blankets are sold with or without vapor barriers.

To insulate an attic floor, lay batts or blankets between the joists. Batts and blankets can be bought with a vapor barrier on one side. To install, place the barrier face down so that, when it is in place, you no longer see it.

To insulate the floor above a basement, push batts or blankets between the floor joists from below. Be sure that the vapor barrier is facing up, towards the house. To support the insulation, lace wire back and forth between nails spaced two feet apart. Or you may tack chicken wire to the joists.

Instead of batts or blankets, you may insulate with loose fill. It is made from glass fiber, rock wool, cellulose, perlite or vermiculite. Loose fill tends to settle after a while. Yet, cellulose, which is made from recycled newspaper, makes an excellent insulator. It must, however, be treated to become fire resistant. Use the loose fill to fill in the spaces between the joists. You will have to put in your own vapor barrier. A plastic sheet may be stapled or tacked down before the loose fill is poured.

Your home may already have some insulation. Even so, you may wish to add some more. In that case here are a few hints. Do not put insulation on top of lighting fixtures for the floor below. Keep insulation at least three inches away from such fixtures. Do not cover eave vents with insulation. Be sure that there is enough space in the attic to let moisture out.

A well-insulated home saves you money. It keeps your home cooler in the summer. It also keeps the house warmer in the winter. Don't be afraid to insulate your home yourself. It's really not a difficult job!

Selection 30: Recalling Facts

1. Which of the following insulations is best installed by a contractor?
   ☐ a. Glass fiber   ☐ b. Plastic foam   ☐ c. Rock wool

2. Batts and blankets come in thicknesses of
   ☐ a. 1 to 7 inches.   ☐ b. 10 to 12 inches.   ☐ c. 15 to 23 inches.

3. Cellulose is made from recycled
   ☐ a. cloth.   ☐ b. plastic.   ☐ c. newspaper.

4. Which of the following is a loose fill insulation?
   ☐ a. Batts   ☐ b. Blankets   ☐ c. Perlite

5. Loose fill should be used to fill the spaces between the
   ☐ a. joists.   ☐ b. shingles.   ☐ c. windows.

Selection 30: Understanding Ideas

6. Many kinds of insulation are
   ☐ a. easy to install.
   ☐ b. expensive to buy.
   ☐ c. harmful to people.

7. The normal spaces in house frames range from
   ☐ a. 1 to 7 inches.
   ☐ b. 8 to 10 inches.
   ☐ c. 15 to 23 inches.

8. If cellulose is not treated, it will
   ☐ a. burn easily.
   ☐ b. dry up.
   ☐ c. hold water.

9. We can see that loose fill does not come with a
   ☐ a. crawl space.   ☐ b. plastic foam.   ☐ c. vapor barrier.

10. A well-insulated house saves you money on your
    ☐ a. food bill.
    ☐ b. heating bill.
    ☐ c. water bill.

31. Think Before You Buy

Reading Time _____

Comprehension Score _____

Words per Minute _____

Before you shop for a carpet for your home, think about colors and textures. What will look good in your home? How long will the carpeting keep its pleasing appearance?

Red, orange and yellow are warm colors. They tend to create a lively and cheery feeling. They are good in rooms that get little sunlight. Also, they can make a large room seem cozier. In a small room, though, they can be overpowering.

Green, blue and violet are cool colors. These colors are useful for sunny rooms or for a formal setting. They tend to make rooms seem cooler and larger.

Gray and beige are neutral. They go well with either warm or cool colors. Neutral colors will blend well with colors already in a room. No matter what color carpet you choose, it will look better in your room if it is part of a planned color scheme.

Single-color schemes are made up of various shades of one color, ranging from light to dark. Use the darkest shade in the carpet and lighter shades in curtains or furniture. Examples of a contrasting-color scheme would be orange with green or blue with yellow. Make one color stand out and have only small things in the contrasting color. If the carpet color contrasts with the walls, the effect will be too much. Use the contrasting color instead in upholstery fabrics.

Texture is important, too. Smooth, even surface textures made of long, closely packed yarns give carpets an expensive look. An uneven texture gives a less formal effect. Patterns or designs can highlight either one of these effects.

Light carpet colors show soil and dust easily. They should not be used if your home has forced-air heat. Air-borne dust will soon darken light colors around air vents. Black, dark brown and other deep colors show lint. A mixture of two or more colors, patterns and designs tends to hide soil. Multi-colored rugs are a wise choice if you don't want your carpet to show the dirt.

Also, even textures tend to show dirt and dust more than uneven textures. Uneven textures, however, are harder to clean and may need more strokes of a vacuum cleaner.

The next time you are in the market for a good carpet, keep these few simple facts in mind. Take time to think about your choice — it will make a world of difference.

Selection 31: Recalling Facts

1. When you choose a carpet for your home, you should think about the rug's color and
    ☐ a. price.　　　　☐ b. texture.　　　　☐ c. weight.

2. Red, orange and yellow are
    ☐ a. cool colors.　　☐ b. sad colors.　　☐ c. warm colors.

3. Green, blue and violet go well in
    ☐ a. a dark room.　　☐ b. a formal setting.　　☐ c. an informal setting.

4. Neutral colors are
    ☐ a. gray and beige.　　☐ b. green and blue.　　☐ c. red and yellow.

5. Light carpet colors should not be used in a home that has
    ☐ a. air conditioning.　　☐ b. forced-air heat.　　☐ c. steam radiators.

Selection 31: Understanding Ideas

6. Red, orange and yellow color schemes can make you feel
    ☐ a. cold.　　　　☐ b. cozy.　　　　☐ c. sad.

7. What colors are best in a small room?
    ☐ a. Red, orange and yellow
    ☐ b. Green, blue and violet
    ☐ c. White, black and gray

8. A room decorated in orange and black is an example of a
    ☐ a. contrasting-color scheme.
    ☐ b. multi-color scheme.
    ☐ c. single-color scheme.

9. A carpet with long, closely packed yarns would probably feel
    ☐ a. coarse.　　　　☐ b. thick.　　　　☐ c. thin.

10. Uneven-textured carpets
    ☐ a. are easy to clean.
    ☐ b. do not show the dirt.
    ☐ c. will not fade or shrink.

32. Ears Are for Listening

Reading Time _____

Comprehension Score _____

Words per Minute _____

A baby spends his first year of life learning to listen. A newborn child comes equipped with a finely-tuned pair of ears, but he doesn't yet know how to use them. A buzz of meaningless noise surrounds him. No one sound means more than any other. Unlike his ears, the hearing center of his brain is still immature. As the baby grows, two things happen. First, he becomes better at picking out certain sounds. Second, he begins to remember them.

This development is easy to see. If you make a loud sound near a day-old baby's head, you will not see any reaction. Only a check on his pulse or breathing rate will show a change. But just two weeks later, the same noise will make him jerk. He may even turn his head toward you. Now the human voice means something to him. If he hears another baby crying, he will cry. By his fourth to sixth week, sounds like the door bell or the closing of a door no longer surprise him. He can pick out one voice — his mother's — from all others. That one voice can soothe him and stop his crying. By eight weeks these mother-sounds can make him smile.

What is actually happening is that he is starting to learn to listen. He can select certain sounds and memorize them. When he hears that sound again, he can match it with the one he has heard before. These skills are basic to all learning.

At the same time these early hearing and language skills get under way, the child begins to practice sound-making. His first sounds are the *discomfort* sounds. These are the shrill whines which he seems to spend all his time making. These sounds are heard when he is not quiet or sleeping. These sounds mean nothing to him yet. To his mother they say that he is wet, or uncomfortable or hungry.

Within the baby's first month, another sound appears: the *comfort* sounds. These are different from the discomfort sounds. These are more throaty and vowel-like. These coos, sighs and grunts are the beginnings of true speech. As the child grows, his comfort sounds will use more of the vowels and consonants and rhythms which he will later use. These sounds will come together to form the first word. An event that will be long remembered by the proud parents.

Selection 32: Recalling Facts

1. A baby spends his first year of life learning
   - ☐ a. to listen.
   - ☐ b. to walk.
   - ☐ c. to run.

2. The first sounds a child makes are called
   - ☐ a. comfort sounds.
   - ☐ b. discomfort sounds.
   - ☐ c. rhythm sounds.

3. The baby's comfort sounds appear around
   - ☐ a. one month.
   - ☐ b. three months.
   - ☐ c. six months.

4. Comfort sounds are
   - ☐ a. musical.
   - ☐ b. shrill.
   - ☐ c. throaty.

5. As the child gets older, he uses more
   - ☐ a. musical tones.
   - ☐ b. throaty sounds.
   - ☐ c. vowels and consonants.

Selection 32: Understanding Ideas

6. A baby learns how to listen before he learns how
   - ☐ a. to eat.
   - ☐ b. to see.
   - ☐ c. to talk.

7. Sound
   - ☐ a. can easily hurt a newborn baby.
   - ☐ b. means nothing to a newborn baby.
   - ☐ c. will put a newborn baby to sleep.

8. We can see that
   - ☐ a. children learn while they sleep.
   - ☐ b. the ears develop before the brain.
   - ☐ c. shrill whines show that the child is happy.

9. If you make a loud noise near a newborn baby, he seems
   - ☐ a. to get angry.
   - ☐ b. to ignore it.
   - ☐ c. to look away.

10. The child needs to practice his sound making in order
    - ☐ a. to listen.
    - ☐ b. sing.
    - ☐ c. to speak.

33. To Your Health

Reading Time _____

Comprehension Score _____

Words per Minute _____

Protein, carbohydrates and fats are needed for a good diet. Along with water and fat, our bodies contain much protein. Protein is most important to a healthy body. Enzymes are made of protein. They help to keep the body working. Antibodies in the blood stream are also made of protein. They fight off disease. The body also needs protein to build muscle. The muscles in turn hold the bone structure together. Muscles provide the strength to move and work. It's a good thing that most of us get enough protein.

But where is protein found? Meat, poultry, fish, milk, cheese and eggs give us good amounts of it. Bread and cereal are also important sources. Vegetables, like soybeans, chickpeas, dry beans and peanuts, are also good sources of protein. You do not have to load up on meat, poultry or eggs to get enough protein in your diet. Eating cereal or vegetable foods with milk, cheese or other animal protein can give you enough protein in your diet. For example, eat cereal with milk, rice with fish, or simply drink a glass of milk during a meal. Together, these foods provide the high quality protein the body needs.

Carbohydrates are the biggest source of energy. This group is made up of starches and sugars. Carbohydrates are mostly found in cereal grains, fruits, vegetables, and sugar. Such foods as wheat, oats, corn and rice provide starch. So, too, do potatoes, sweet potatoes and vegetables like peas, dry beans, peanuts and soybeans. Most other vegetables have smaller amounts of carbohydrates. In vegetables, the carbohydrates are usually in the form of starch. In fruits, they show up as sugar. Of course, candies, jams and syrups are mostly sugar.

Fats give us energy. They add flavor and variety to foods. They make meals more satisfying. Fats carry vitamins A, D, E and K. Fats are also an important part of the cells which make up the body's tissues. Our body fat protects our important organs by surrounding them with a cushion. Fats are found in butter, margarine, shortening, salad oils, and cream. Most cheeses, mayonnaise, salad dressing, nuts and bacon also have a good deal of fat.

A good and balanced diet will use foods from all three of the above groups. In the end, eating right pays off in a healthier body. You'll not only look better, but you will also feel better.

Selection 33: Recalling Facts

1. Protein, carbohydrates and fats are needed for a good
   □ a. diet.　　　　□ b. job.　　　　□ c. rest.

2. Antibodies are found in the
   □ a. brain.　　　　□ b. blood.　　　　□ c. heart.

3. Antibodies fight off
   □ a. calories.　　　　□ b. disease.　　　　□ c. fat.

4. Which of the following is a good source of protein?
   □ a. Butter　　　　□ b. Meat　　　　□ c. Sugar

5. What is the biggest source of energy in our diet?
   □ a. Carbohydrates　　　　□ b. Protein　　　　□ c. Vitamins

Selection 33: Understanding Ideas

6. If we did not have antibodies in our blood, we would probably become
   □ a. overweight.　　　　□ b. sick.　　　　□ c. tired.

7. Our bones are held together by
   □ a. fats.　　　　□ b. muscles.　　　　□ c. protein.

8. Fats are used by our bodies
   □ a. to build muscles.
   □ b. to carry antibodies.
   □ c. to protect our organs.

9. Soybeans are a source of both protein and
   □ a. carbohydrates.　　　　□ b. minerals.　　　　□ c. vitamins.

10. What is this article about?
    □ a. Disease, infection and germs
    □ b. Protein, carbohydrates and fats
    □ c. Vitamins, minerals and protein

34. A Change Is Near

Reading Time _____

Comprehension Score _____

Words per Minute _____

The United States has joined the trend toward a system of measurement called the metric system. The names of the units in this system may sound strange to our ears. Still, there are only a few words that we have to learn for daily use. Some units of measure that we now use will not change. Time will still be measured in hours, minutes and seconds. Electric power will still be measured in watts. Our money system will stay the same.

The metric system is already being used in this country. In swimming, track and field events, lengths are given in meters rather than in yards and feet. Our astronauts told the world how far their rocket had landed from a lunar hill in meters. You see weights listed in grams on more and more packaged items at the market. The trend toward metric is increasing.

The metric system is becoming popular throughout the world for two reasons. One, it is a simple system. Two, it is a decimal system. It is simple because each quantity, such as length (meter) or weight (gram), has its own unit of measure. No unit is used to show more than one quantity. In the system we now use, pounds can mean force, as in pounds needed to break a rope. Pounds can also be used for weight, as in a pound of sugar. Ounce can mean volume, as the number of ounces in a quart. Ounce can be used for weight, as the number of ounces in a pound.

The metric system is easier to learn to use in solving problems. This is because metric units are related to each other. They are based on a factor of 10. This makes figuring an easy task.

Think about the measurement of length. In the metric system, a measure of length is shown in meters or multiples of the meter. A centimeter is one hundredth of a meter. A millimeter is one thousandth of a meter. A kilometer is one thousand meters. All units are either a division or a multiple of 10.

More and more we will see the use of metrics. Children are now taught the metric system in school. Road signs on the highways will soon give distances in kilometers. More consumer goods will be made and labeled using metric units. The change is coming. Soon metric units will no longer be strange to our ears.

81

Selection 34: Recalling Facts

1. Which of the following units of measure will not change under the metric system?
   - ☐ a. Distance
   - ☐ b. Time
   - ☐ c. Weight

2. In track and field events, lengths are given in
   - ☐ a. grams.
   - ☐ b. liters.
   - ☐ c. meters.

3. The metric system is becoming popular because it is
   - ☐ a. hard.
   - ☐ b. large.
   - ☐ c. simple.

4. Metric units are based on a multiple of
   - ☐ a. 4.
   - ☐ b. 10.
   - ☐ c. 12.

5. A kilometer equals
   - ☐ a. ten meters.
   - ☐ b. one hundred meters.
   - ☐ c. one thousand meters.

Selection 34: Understanding Ideas

6. What is the main idea of this article?
   - ☐ a. The metric system has an interesting history.
   - ☐ b. Soon everyone will be using the metric system.
   - ☐ c. The United States refuses to use metric measure.

7. This article hints that under the metric system
   - ☐ a. astronauts will not fly.
   - ☐ b. some units will not change.
   - ☐ c. things will weigh more.

8. Yards and feet measure
   - ☐ a. length.
   - ☐ b. volume.
   - ☐ c. weight.

9. This article hints that
   - ☐ a. children are not able to learn the metric system.
   - ☐ b. it is easier to solve problems using the metric system.
   - ☐ c. the metric system is mostly used in South America.

10. A kilometer measures
    - ☐ a. length.
    - ☐ b. sound.
    - ☐ c. volume.

35. A Stitch in Time

Reading Time _____

Comprehension Score _____

Words per Minute _____

Fibers have been used for making cloth for thousands of years. Many of them are still used today to make fabric. Linen, for example, is the oldest textile fabric. It comes from the flax plant. It was used in prehistoric times and in ancient Egypt. We have learned that linen was woven in England as early as the year 400. Today this fiber is used in many ways around the home. In fact, the word "linens" has come to be used as the name for household textile goods, such as sheets and towels.

Wool, also, dates back as far as Bible times. Much later, in the 15th and 16th centuries, sheep from Spain and England were brought to the American colonies. Spanish explorers brought sheep with them from California to Florida. Thus, wool came to be used here in America.

Another leading fiber is cotton. It was woven into fabrics in India as early as 1500 years before Christ. Cotton was also used for candle wicks in England as far back as the 1300s. By the 1400s, cotton fabrics were being manufactured in central Europe. In 1793 in the southern United States, Eli Whitney invented the "cotton engine." This name was later shortened to become the "cotton gin." It was used to comb seeds out of cotton fibers. This machine removed a major delay in the processing of cotton. Because of it, cotton became the South's most important crop.

The production of silk began with the ancient Chinese. Legend says that a Chinese empress saw a silkworm spinning its cocoon. The empress wondered how she would look in a gown made of such fine material. Silk weaving soon spread. It was seen in many other countries. But silkworm raising remained wholly Chinese until the sixth century. At that time, the art spread to other parts of the Middle East.

The fibers that have been mentioned so far are all natural. But today there are many man-made fibers in use. Some of these were made for a certain need. Others were discovered mostly by chance. Production of man-made fiber was chiefly a United States industry until the 1950s. After the 1950s things changed. Foreign production grew until, by 1960, this country made less than half of the world's man-made fibers. Rayon and nylon are just a few examples of today's man-made fabrics.

Selection 35: Recalling Facts

1. The oldest textile fabric is
   □ a. cotton.   □ b. linen.   □ c. silk.

2. Wool was brought from California to Florida by the
   □ a. American Indians.
   □ b. French traders.
   □ c. Spanish explorers.

3. Cotton was woven into fabrics in India as early as
   □ a. Columbus's first voyage.
   □ b. the late 1300s.
   □ c. 1500 years before Christ.

4. Silk production began with the
   □ a. ancient Chinese.
   □ b. early Spanish colonists.
   □ c. first English explorers.

5. Which of the following is a man-made fiber?
   □ a. Cotton   □ b. Linen   □ c. Rayon

Selection 35: Understanding Ideas

6. Which of the following is most likely true?
   □ a. American colonists did not know how to weave.
   □ b. Linen is an extremely old fabric.
   □ c. The Spanish were the first to use silk.

7. Wool comes from
   □ a. an animal.   □ b. a mineral.   □ c. a plant.

8. This article hints that
   □ a. cotton was used in India before it was used in America.
   □ b. the southern United States once raised many sheep.
   □ c. no one knows how the flax plant came to America.

9. Silk comes from
   □ a. an animal.   □ b. a plant.   □ c. a vitamin.

10. We can see from this article that fabrics
    □ a. are costly to make and ship.
    □ b. can be natural or man-made.
    □ c. change with the fashion.

36. Think Thin

Reading Time _____

Comprehension Score _____

Words per Minute _____

Persons who are overweight should watch their diet carefully in order to lose pounds. The best way to do this is to start a weight control program. At first it is wise to talk with your doctor. He can tell you if your health is good enough for you to try to lose weight. If you are in good health, your doctor can tell you how much weight you should lose. He can advise you of the number of calories you should have in your meals each day. He can tell you about exercising while on your diet. A good rule is to lose slowly. A loss of a pound or two a week is plenty.

Plans meals around foods you know. The best diet for you is the one you can be faithful to. This means that it is wise to include foods that you are used to and that are part of your regular eating habits. Strange foods may not satisfy you. They may throw you off your diet. When you have lost the weight you wish, simple items can be added to your diet so that you can maintain the weight you want. While you are dieting, try to build a pattern of eating that you can follow later to maintain your desired weight. Strange and glamorous foods used on a diet may work but will be hard to continue eating afterwards. As a result, you may become discouraged and go back to your old habits that put on the extra weight in the first place.

When you plan meals, follow a sound food plan. Be sure to include the daily nutrition you need. Make certain you are getting the right kinds of food.

When dieting, choose low-calorie foods. Avoid such items as fats, gravy, sauce, fried food, sweets, cakes, alcoholic drinks or soft drinks, and cream. Use spices, herbs or tart fruit juices to season your food.

Learn to like cereal or fruit with little or no sugar added. Try to take coffee and tea without sugar or cream. Snacks can be part of your diet. For example, a piece of fruit or crisp vegetable, or a simple dessert saved from mealtime, can be eaten between meals.

Keep busy! This way you will not be tempted to go off the diet. Take advantage of opportunities to exercise. Try walking instead of riding whenever possible. Happy dieting!

Selection 36: Recalling Facts

1. The first thing to do if you want to lose weight is
    - ☐ a. stop eating breakfast.
    - ☐ b. talk to your doctor.
    - ☐ c. weigh yourself daily.

2. What is the most you should lose a week?
    - ☐ a. One or two pounds
    - ☐ b. Five or six pounds
    - ☐ c. Ten or twelve pounds

3. When dieting you should choose
    - ☐ a. high-protein foods.
    - ☐ b. high-starch foods.
    - ☐ c. low-calorie foods.

4. Which of the following should be included in a good diet?
    - ☐ a. Alcoholic drinks   ☐ b. Crisp vegetables   ☐ c. Fried foods

5. A good diet snack would be a
    - ☐ a. candy bar.   ☐ b. piece of fruit.   ☐ c. sweet cake.

Selection 36: Understanding Ideas

6. This article tells us
    - ☐ a. about fad diets.   ☐ b. how to diet.   ☐ c. why we should diet.

7. Which of the following would *not* be a good diet food?
    - ☐ a. Carrots   ☐ b. French fries   ☐ c. Steak

8. This article suggests that when you diet you should also
    - ☐ a. exercise.   ☐ b. fast.   ☐ c. relax.

9. What can we conclude from this article?
    - ☐ a. Doctors do not like to put people on diets.
    - ☐ b. Only people who are in good health should diet.
    - ☐ c. Weight control is not necessary for overweight people.

10. Tart fruit juices can be used
    - ☐ a. to clean foods.   ☐ b. to flavor foods.   ☐ c. to preserve foods.

37. A Smart Shopper

Reading Time _____

Comprehension Score _____

Words per Minute _____

Where you do your major food shopping often affects your grocery bill. It's best to check the price in nearby stores for the foods you buy all the time. You can then decide which store gives you the best prices. Check, too, for other features that may be useful to you. Which store offers the freshest foods? Which store has off-street parking and will cash your check?

Small stores will deliver orders to your home. If you do not need this service, you will do better shopping at a large chain. The large chain markets offer more variety and have better prices.

For most people it is best to choose a store with good prices and stay with it. Store-hopping for sales on certain foods may save you pennies, but it can be costly in time and gas.

When you shop depends on your schedule. Try to go when the store is not too crowded and when you have time to choose with care. Study labels and compare prices. Learn about new products. Give food buying all the attention it deserves.

The meat, poultry, and fish items in your menu usually cost the most. Studies show that one-third of the money spent on food goes for these items. To take advantage of the best buys at the meat counter, you need to be aware of the many cuts of meat that are available. Also, you must know how to use them in meals. Keep in mind that the economy of a cut depends on the amount of cooked lean meat it serves as well as its price per pound. Often the cut with a low price per pound is not the best buy. What counts is the amount of lean meat and the number of servings it will provide. For example, a high-priced meat with little or no waste may be a better buy than a low-priced cut with a great deal of bone or fat.

Same-size servings of cooked lean meat from different types and cuts of meat often have the same food value. As a rule, cooked lean meat from pot roast is as nutritious as that from steak. Fish has as much nutrition as lamb, and turkey has as much as veal. So when you visit the market, be a smart shopper and take the time to make the right choice.

Selection 37: Recalling Facts

1. For foods you buy all the time, it is good to check different stores to find the best
   □ a. cashiers. □ b. prices. □ c. registers.

2. Store-hopping wastes
   □ a. groceries. □ b. clothes. □ c. time.

3. When choosing a product carefully, you should look at the price and the
   □ a. cashiers. □ b. carriage. □ c. label.

4. One-third of the grocery bill is spent on
   □ a. cheese, milk and eggs.
   □ b. meat, poultry and fish.
   □ c. vegetables and fruits.

5. Cooked lean pot roast is just as nutritious as
   □ a. potatoes. □ b. steak. □ c. sugar.

Selection 37: Understanding Ideas

6. Large chain markets do *not*
   □ a. have a large variety of foods.
   □ b. offer the freshest foods.
   □ c. make home grocery deliveries.

7. We can see that store-hopping
   □ a. is often the sign of a wise shopper.
   □ b. may cost you more money than it saves.
   □ c. will cut down on your grocery bill.

8. This article hints that meat
   □ a. is expensive. □ b. is not nutritious. □ c. spoils easily.

9. A cheap cut of meat may not be as good a buy as a
   □ a. heavily salted cut.
   □ b. more expensive cut.
   □ c. well-packaged cut.

10. What is the main idea of this article?
    □ a. Careful food shopping can save you money.
    □ b. Large food markets have small parking lots.
    □ c. Small food stores are very scarce.

38. Let's Solve
That Problem Together

When a youngster is faced with a problem, he may not be able to deal with it. He needs help to learn how. When a puzzle piece doesn't fit, or when an ice cream cone falls onto the ground, he turns to someone older for help. If you want to help someone learn problem-solving skills, you should take the time to talk about problems as they happen. Of course, this is not always easy to do. Problems have a way of popping up at the worst times. Even if the time is not the best, you should try to help.

One thing you can do to help a youngster develop problem-solving skills is to find out what caused the problem. This is a skill that youngsters do not learn without help. For example, a youngster may knock over his glass of milk at the dinner table. The child may not realize that the problem is that the glass is too close to his elbow. But, once the problem is seen for what it is, it can be solved.

The next step for a youngster is to choose a solution. This step takes courage. Some people are so afraid of being wrong that they cannot solve problems. You can help by talking over some solutions to the problem. Between the two of you, decide which solution is the best and let the youngster try it out. You can help him realize that problems can be solved. Give him the courage and praise he needs to try his solution.

Another step to problem-solving is to help youngsters see the laws of cause and effect. For example, if the child knocks over a vase, it will fall and break. If he writes on the wall, it will leave a mark. Once the youngster sees the relationship between cause and effect, he is on the road to growth. The next time he sees someone knock over a vase, he knows it will break. If he sees writing on the wall, he can tell how it got there.

The ability to deal with problems does not come easily for youngsters. It does not come easily for adults, either. It takes patience for you. It takes practice for the youngster. It can be a tiring experience, but problem-solving can be taught. All it takes is time and effort.

Selection 38: Recalling Facts

1. In order to teach problem-solving skills, you should take the time to talk about problems
   - ☐ a. before they happen.
   - ☐ b. as they happen.
   - ☐ c. after they happen.

2. One way to help a youngster solve a problem is
   - ☐ a. to find out the cause.
   - ☐ b. to forget the problem.
   - ☐ c. to punish the child.

3. In order for a child to choose a solution, he needs
   - ☐ a. courage.   ☐ b. honesty.   ☐ c. talent.

4. One step to problem-solving is to help the youngster see the laws of
   - ☐ a. cause and effect.   ☐ b. space and distance.   ☐ c. time and sequence.

5. Problem-solving is a skill that can be
   - ☐ a. forgotten.   ☐ b. ignored.   ☐ c. learned.

Selection 38: Understanding Ideas

6. The writer makes this article clear by using
   - ☐ a. examples.   ☐ b. graphs.   ☐ c. numbers.

7. Problem solving
   - ☐ a. is not easy.   ☐ b. is not a skill.   ☐ c. is not taught.

8. This article suggests that
   - ☐ a. anyone can learn to solve problems.
   - ☐ b. children can easily solve their own problems.
   - ☐ c. most problems cannot be solved.

9. When an adult and a child try to choose a solution to a problem, they should
   - ☐ a. begin by discussing the different solutions.
   - ☐ b. disagree about its solutions.
   - ☐ c. try to find out who is to blame.

10. According to this article,
    - ☐ a. it takes practice and patience to solve problems.
    - ☐ b. people often make their own problems.
    - ☐ c. the problems that occur daily are easy to solve.

39. Cozy Covers

Reading Time _____

Comprehension Score _____

Words per Minute _____

There is a short supply of oil in the world today. This shortage has caused changes in the way we all live. For example, over 45 million American homes now use electric blankets for sleeping at night. The cost of using an electric blanket is small. On a medium setting the cost is no more than half a cent for all night.

Few people know that an electric blanket does not heat you up at night. The truth is that the blanket stops the loss of body heat. The blanket provides a warm layer of air which keeps the heat in. The body itself does most of the work.

However, life was not always so cozy beneath the covers. People once shivered as they slept. To keep warm, early man used animal hides and campfires. Later on, fireplaces and wool blankets were used. Around 1600 another improvement came onto the scene. This aid was the warming pan. Hot coals were put into a shallow pan, and the pan was moved around under the covers to warm the bed. Still later someone invented the feather-filled comforter. This new kind of blanket used the body heat to warm the bed.

But the first real breakthrough came when boilers were brought into the home in the 19th century. Radiators were used to heat each room. This also meant that the heat for the entire home could be controlled. Quite a welcomed improvement.

Then, in the late 1800s, electric blankets came on the scene. They arrived just after the boilers. But these early blankets were not meant to give comfort to the user. Rather, they were part of medical treatment. At that time, doctors felt that the more painful the cure, the better it was for the patient. Electric blankets were used to make the patient sweat. Sweating rid the body of germs.

Hospitals, then, were among the first to use the new blankets. Sometimes patients had to sleep outdoors on porches. The blankets were used to protect them from cold and snow. There is no record of the number of patients who survived this treatment. But in this case the cure was probably more uncomfortable than the illness.

Electric blankets now come in all sizes. They are light, warm and easy to keep clean. Today they are sold in large quantities. It seems we've come a long way since buffalo hides and warming pans. So, let's hear it for modern inventions that make life more comfortable.

Selection 39: Recalling Facts

1. How many American homes now use electric blankets?
   - ☐ a. About 10 million
   - ☐ b. Around 30 million
   - ☐ c. Over 45 million

2. What is the nightly cost of using an electric blanket?
   - ☐ a. Half a cent
   - ☐ b. A nickel
   - ☐ c. Twelve cents

3. An electric blanket keeps you warm by preventing a loss of body
   - ☐ a. fat.
   - ☐ b. fluid.
   - ☐ c. heat.

4. The warming pan came into use around
   - ☐ a. 1400.
   - ☐ b. 1500.
   - ☐ c. 1600.

5. Radiators were invented in the
   - ☐ a. 15th century.
   - ☐ b. 19th century.
   - ☐ c. 20th century.

Selection 39: Understanding Ideas

6. This article hints that electric blankets
   - ☐ a. are dangerous.
   - ☐ b. save energy.
   - ☐ c. stop disease.

7. Today more people are using electric blankets because of
   - ☐ a. their bright colors.
   - ☐ b. the oil shortage.
   - ☐ c. their low price.

8. We can see that early man had trouble keeping
   - ☐ a. clean.
   - ☐ b. healthy.
   - ☐ c. warm.

9. The feather-filled comforter was a better invention than
   - ☐ a. electric blankets.
   - ☐ b. radiators.
   - ☐ c. warming pans.

10. Electric blankets were once used
    - ☐ a. to decorate floors.
    - ☐ b. to cure sick people.
    - ☐ c. to cover tables.

40. Lend an Ear

Reading Time _____

Comprehension Score _____

Words per Minute _____

Noise is ear pollution. It is often called "unwanted sound." If a sound is something you like, a song or a call from a friend, it is just a sound. But if you are trying to sleep or study, then this sound becomes a noise.

This "unwanted sound" has an effect upon our bodies. For example, loud noises can cause a loss of hearing. Even wanted sound, such as amplified rock-and-roll music, can hurt your hearing, though you may not think of it as noise. The first warning that a sound may be loud enough to hurt is called "ear distress." This would be felt as a pain or heard as a ringing noise in the ear. People who have this complaint should be examined by a doctor.

Noise of any kind may make you nervous or affect your sleep. Noise can also affect your speech and your ability to think. Noise has been linked to cases of heart disease, ulcers, mental illness, and other sicknesses.

Noise, of course, is not always bad. It does have a place in our lives. You may not like to hear car horns, but they do warn you of oncoming cars when you cross a street. A thumping noise from a bicycle tire tells you that the tire may be flat. Also, one noise can help block out another unwanted noise. An example is when loud music in an office drowns out the sounds of typewriters.

Sound is made by air pressure on your eardrums. When you clap your hands, for example, listen to the sound. Air was pushed out from between your hands when you brought them together. At almost the same time, air in your ears pushed your eardrums inward. Your ears signaled your brain to give you the feeling of a clap sound.

The number of sound waves hitting your eardrums each second controls the highness or lowness of the sound you hear. The strength of sound waves is measured by a sound level meter. The meter uses units called decibels. A whisper amounts to about 20 decibels. A jet plane 100 feet away is about 140 decibels. A sound of about 120 decibels can hurt the ears. Eventually, the ear becomes damaged from such loud noises. It's a good thing that the average speaking voice reaches only 60 decibels. Otherwise, we might all be a little deaf.

Selection 40: Recalling Facts

1. Noise is often called
   □ a. expected sound. □ b. air pollution. □ c. unwanted sound.

2. Loud noises can cause
   □ a. death. □ b. a loss of hearing. □ c. poor eyesight.

3. Sound is made by air pressure on your
   □ a. eardrums. □ b. lungs. □ c. throat.

4. The strength of a whisper is about
   □ a. 20 decibels. □ b. 40 decibels. □ c. 60 decibels.

5. The sound of a jet plane 100 feet away measures about
   □ a. 100 decibels. □ b. 120 decibels. □ c. 140 decibels.

Selection 40: Understanding Ideas

6. This article is about
   □ a. ear pollution.
   □ b. jet plane noises.
   □ c. sound level meters.

7. Listening to amplified rock-and-roll music can result in
   □ a. lack of balance.
   □ b. slight hearing loss.
   □ c. a weight gain.

8. The writer hints that
   □ a. noise can cause illness.
   □ b. many people are born deaf.
   □ c. sound is always pleasing.

9. We hear when the ear sends a message to the
   □ a. brain. □ b. eyes. □ c. heart.

10. Noises that are over 120 decibels are
    □ a. harmful. □ b. helpful. □ c. peaceful.

41. Beware the Air

Can you see the sky clearly where you live? If not, the air may be polluted. Polluted air can smell bad or look smoky. But pollution could also be there without your smelling or seeing it.

Air pollution comes from soot, fly ash and chemicals. These are released by auto exhaust, chimney smoke, burning garbage dumps, and substances sprayed in the air. Soot from burning fuel oil is the main pollutant that gives smoke its dark color. Fly ash is tiny ashes that go up and out of chimneys. They make smoke even darker. Chemicals of many kinds that you cannot see mix with the smoke. Smog, the eye-stinging haze that hangs over most cities, is produced when chemicals in the air mix with sunlight.

Air pollutants, such as soot and fly ash, settle down on things and make them dirty. Blown by the wind, air pollutants act like sandpaper and scratch away buildings and statues. Chemical air pollutants discolor and eat away materials. Can you find any change in the color of bricks on old buildings near where you live? Is there a statue in the park that is crumbling away? If you find these things, chances are that air pollution was one of the causes.

Plants are also harmed by air pollution. Their leaves may get dry. Brown spots may appear on them. Or the leaves may turn yellow and fall off. Orange and other citrus trees are especially hurt. Even house plants suffer from air pollution from cooking fumes.

Animals are also affected by air pollution. Cattle can get sick, and so can pets. For example, a small amount of some chemicals sprayed near an aquarium may kill pet fish. Care must be taken so that you and your pets are safe from fumes. Harmful fumes can come from many places. Fumes from paints, lotions, glue, cleaning fluids and other chemicals can be harmful.

Even a little air pollution can make your eyes burn and your head ache. It can tire you out. It can blur your vision and make you dizzy. It can also make it hard for you to breathe. Air pollutants can also affect people with asthma. It can make catching colds and flu more likely. Air pollutants have even been linked to some cases of serious diseases, such as lung cancer and heart ailments, thus making air pollution an evil to beware of.

Selection 41: Recalling Facts

1. Air pollution comes from soot, fly ash and
   - □ a. chemicals.
   - □ b. litter.
   - □ c. sunlight.

2. What gives smoke its dark color?
   - □ a. Charcoal
   - □ b. Pollen
   - □ c. Soot

3. Tiny ashes that go up and out the chimney are called
   - □ a. fly ash.
   - □ b. fly aways.
   - □ c. fly soot.

4. The eye-stinging haze that hangs over most cities is called
   - □ a. ash.
   - □ b. fog.
   - □ c. smog.

5. Materials can be eaten away and discolored by
   - □ a. chemical air pollutants.
   - □ b. cooking fumes.
   - □ c. untreated sewage.

Selection 41: Understanding Ideas

6. Polluted air
   - □ a. helps to put out fires.
   - □ b. may not smell bad.
   - □ c. is good for plants.

7. Which of the following causes air pollution?
   - □ a. Automobiles
   - □ b. Plants
   - □ c. Sunlight

8. Chemical air pollutants
   - □ a. can destroy buildings.
   - □ b. can help people with asthma.
   - □ c. can make plants grow.

9. Cooking fumes can be harmful to
   - □ a. house plants.
   - □ b. nearby neighbors.
   - □ c. small infants.

10. We can see that air pollution
    - □ a. can make you sick.
    - □ b. is not very common.
    - □ c. may help cure the common cold.

42. What to Do?

Reading Time _____

Comprehension Score _____

Words per Minute _____

What happens to all the solid waste produced in the United States? Well, some of it is thrown away. It litters streets, roadways, the countryside and waterways. Some of it is burned in open air. Still some trash is left to sit in the open at garbage dumps. These dumps smell, look bad and attract rats and insects. Some of the trash is buried. Valuable materials that might have been reclaimed and reused are thus lost. Some of the buried waste can be harmful. It leaks deadly chemicals which poison the land and the water.

Waste is everywhere. Each year we throw away more than 7 million television sets. We junk 7 million old cars and trucks. We use and discard 48 billion cans and 26 billion bottles. We toss out 30 million tons of paper. Waste disposal costs us four and a half billion dollars a year. Something has to be done with all this trash and garbage. Even though we are not sure of the best way to get rid of trash, we must make an effort.

Open garbage dumps are the most common place we put our solid wastes. Therefore, it's a good place to start. These dumps can be made better by turning them into clean landfills. In such a landfill, a layer of soil is applied daily over the waste. This helps to keep pests away and cuts down on the water pollutants that wash off in the rain A landfill does away with the need to burn the waste, and this prevents wind-blown litter. When filled, the site can be planted with grass, shrubs and trees and made into a park.

But ordinary sanitary landfills may not stop waste matter from seeping through the soil and ruining water supplies. Dangerous waste matter needs landfills that are sealed in a special way to stop seepage. In the past harmful waste was burned. It was also dumped into waterways. But then pollution controls went into effect. More of these wastes showed up in landfills. The yearly amount of harmful waste is on the rise. Our health is threatened by the unsafe waste from these landfills.

There are good ways to get rid of most dangerous waste without harming health or the ecology. But costs of such disposal are high. Federal and state governments are working with business firms and citizens to solve these cost and waste problems.

Selection 42: Recalling Facts

1. Open dumps attract
   - ☐ a. game animals.
   - ☐ b. rats and insects.
   - ☐ c. trash collectors.

2. Some of the buried waste has deadly
   - ☐ a. chemicals.
   - ☐ b. insects.
   - ☐ c. plants.

3. How many junk cars are thrown away each year?
   - ☐ a. 7 million
   - ☐ b. 26 billion
   - ☐ c. 30 billion

4. Garbage dumps can be made better by turning them into
   - ☐ a. clean landfills.
   - ☐ b. parking lots.
   - ☐ c. usable canals.

5. The yearly amount of harmful waste is
   - ☐ a. decreasing.
   - ☐ b. increasing.
   - ☐ c. stable.

Selection 42: Understanding Ideas

6. Open garbage dumps are
   - ☐ a. beautiful.
   - ☐ b. dangerous.
   - ☐ c. restful ·

7. We can see that many people
   - ☐ a. have open garbage dumps in their yards.
   - ☐ b. save millions of tons of newspapers.
   - ☐ c. throw away things that can be reused.

8. A clean landfill takes the place of
   - ☐ a. a beautiful park.
   - ☐ b. an open garbage dump.
   - ☐ c. an unpolluted waterway.

9. Getting rid of waste is
   - ☐ a. easy.
   - ☐ b. expensive.
   - ☐ c. unpopular.

10. This article hints that
    - ☐ a. litter along the highway is usually cleaned up by the town.
    - ☐ b. more and more people are concerned with waste disposal.
    - ☐ c. waste disposal is not an important problem.

43. Best Buy for Your Money

Reading Time _____

Comprehension Score _____

Words per Minute _____

Most breads and cereals are well liked. They are cheap and fit easily into meal plans. Some cost just cents per serving. Even though they are cheap, the whole grain or enriched products have good amounts of vitamins and minerals. One food study showed that just 12 cents of each food dollar went for flour, cereals and bakery products.

To help you get your money's worth from breads and cereals, there are some things you should keep in mind. Whole-grain or enriched foods have much more nutrition than unenriched products. Most white bread is enriched. Some special breads, such as French, Italian, and raisin, and many other bake shop products are also enriched. Check the wrapper or ask the baker to be sure.

You should also know that it takes three pounds of unenriched bread, costing more than $1, to give the amount of thiamin that is contained in one pound of enriched bread, costing 25 cents. The same is true of whole wheat bread, which costs only 40 cents for one pound. Also, a large loaf of bread does not always weigh more or contain more food value than a small loaf. Compare prices of equal *weights* of bread to find the better buy. The weight is shown on the wrapper.

Spaghetti, macaroni and noodles in packages marked "enriched" are more nutritious and usually cost no more than unenriched ones. Enriched rice is more nutritious than white milled rice. It costs more but the extra food value it provides is well worth the cost.

Ready-to-serve cereals in packs of small boxes are expensive. They may cost two or three times as much per ounce as the same cereal in a large box. Pre-sugared cereals cost more per ounce than unsweetened ones. Sugared cereals have more calories but less food value. Cereals you sweeten yourself are a better buy. Cereals you cook yourself almost always cost less than the ready-prepared ones.

It may help to know that day-old bread and baked goods may be bought at a great saving. Ask or watch for these in stores where you shop. Baked goods made at home are a good idea. They often cost less than ready-baked products. When made at home with enriched flour, they may have more nutrition, too.

So the next time you shop, make sure you are getting the most nutrition for the least money.

Selection 43: Recalling Facts

1. How much out of every food dollar goes for flour, cereals and bakery products?
   ☐ a. 12 cents   ☐ b. 50 cents   ☐ c. 64 cents

2. Unenriched products are not as nutritious as
   ☐ a. milled foods.   ☐ b. packaged foods.   ☐ c. whole-grain foods.

3. How many pounds of unenriched bread does it take to give the amount of thiamin in one pound of enriched bread?
   ☐ a. Two   ☐ b. Three   ☐ c. Four

4. Whole wheat bread costs about
   ☐ a. 25 cents a pound.   ☐ b. 40 cents a pound.   ☐ c. 55 cents a pound.

5. To make sure a product is enriched, you should check the
   ☐ a. price.   ☐ b. store.   ☐ c. wrapper.

Selection 43: Understanding Ideas

6. What is the main idea of this passage?
   ☐ a. Breads and cereals fit well into most diets.
   ☐ b. Milled rice is not as nutritious as enriched rice.
   ☐ c. Ready-baked products are not very expensive.

7. This article hints that
   ☐ a. breads and cereals are expensive.
   ☐ b. unenriched foods are high in vitamins.
   ☐ c. whole-grain foods are nutritious.

8. When checking bread to find the better buy, make sure the breads are the same
   ☐ a. price.   ☐ b. length.   ☐ c. weight.

9. Pre-sugared cereals
   ☐ a. are just as nutritious as enriched cereals.
   ☐ b. are not very popular with most parents.
   ☐ c. are not as nutritious as unsweetened cereals.

10. When you bake homemade pastry, it's a good idea to use
    ☐ a. brown sugar.   ☐ b. enriched flour.   ☐ c. milled rice.

44. Happy Home Buying

Reading Time _____

Comprehension Score _____

Words per Minute _____

You have found a home you want to buy. What is the next step? Very likely you will need a mortgage loan to pay for your home. Most families do pay a good part of the purchase price of a home with a mortgage.

A mortgage is a loan contract. A bank agrees to provide the money you need to buy a certain home. You, in turn, agree to repay the money based on terms stated in the agreement.

The size of each payment depends on three things. The first is the amount of money you have borrowed. The second thing is the interest rate charged by the bank. The third thing is the number of years you need to pay the loan off. Under law, the contract has to state the amount of the loan, the interest you will pay, and the size and times of the payments. Any other charges made by the bank must also be included in the contract.

As the borrower, you must promise your home as security for the loan. It remains pledged until the loan is paid off. If you fail to meet the terms of the contract, the bank has the right to foreclose. Under the law, this means that the bank can take your home and sell it to pay off the loan.

Most mortgages are installment loans. This means that you are required to make a fixed payment — usually once a month. Part of the payment is kept by the bank to cover the interest charges. Part of it may be set aside by the bank to pay your taxes and insurance. And part of the payment reduces the principal of the loan. The principal is the actual amount that you borrowed.

In the beginning, most of each payment goes for the interest. As you keep paying, a smaller share of each payment is for interest and a larger share repays the principal. As your payments reduce the amount you owe on the principal of the loan, the interest charges are reduced.

You build up equity in your home as you pay off the mortgage. Equity is that part of your home which you own free from the bank. When the last payment on the mortgage is made, you will have full equity. The home will be completely yours. The interest has been paid off. The principal has been repaid in full.

Selection 44: Recalling Facts

1. In order to pay for a new home, you must apply for
   ☐ a. an account. ☐ b. a job. ☐ c. a loan.

2. A mortgage is a
   ☐ a. checking account. ☐ b. loan contract. ☐ c. tax return.

3. Which of the following is *not* included in a mortgage payment?
   ☐ a. Interest charge ☐ b. Service charge ☐ c. Taxes

4. The actual amount borrowed is called the
   ☐ a. contract. ☐ b. principal. ☐ c. repayment.

5. That part of your home that you own free from the bank is called
   ☐ a. equity. ☐ b. insurance. ☐ c. security.

Selection 44: Understanding Ideas

6. This article hints that
   ☐ a. banks will not lend money to families.
   ☐ b. many people borrow money to buy a house.
   ☐ c. older homes are not worth buying.

7. We can guess from this article that
   ☐ a. banks don't like to give mortgages.
   ☐ b. mortgage payments vary greatly.
   ☐ c. new houses don't need insurance.

8. If you do not meet your monthly payments, the bank has the right
   ☐ a. to decorate your home.
   ☐ b. to destroy your home.
   ☐ c. to sell your home.

9. During the first few years of paying a mortgage, most of your monthly payment goes for
   ☐ a. interest. ☐ b. taxes. ☐ c. insurance.

10. When is your equity in your home the greatest?
   ☐ a. Before you begin your payments
   ☐ b. During the first few years of your payments
   ☐ c. Toward the end of your payments

45. Child Proofing

Reading Time _____

Comprehension Score _____

Words per Minute _____

Poisonings which cause death happen most of the time to children between the ages of one and three. Some doctors call this stage the "Age of Accidents." Children want to look at things and taste them. They will eat or drink anything they can find, even if it tastes bad. You must make your home safe for children and protect them from poisoning.

Here are three things you can do. One, know which things around the home are poisons. Two, keep poisons out of your child's reach at all times. Three, be aware of how clever children are when it comes to finding poisons.

Nearly all chemicals and drugs in the home contain things which can poison some-one. Be sure to read the labels on products you bring into the home. Look for the words which are meant as warnings. These warnings will read *Poison, Harmful if Swallowed, For External Use Only,* and *Keep Out of Reach of Children.* Look around your home for bottles and jars which bear these warnings. Then, put them away in a place where a child cannot reach or find them.

You should know that you cannot always rely on the label on a product to give you the proper warning. There are things such as nail polish, perfume, make-up, hair tonic and others which give you no clue to the dangers that might result from swallowing. Drinks with alcohol, such as gin, whiskey, beer, and wine, do not carry warnings. These, too, can cause your child harm. You cannot know which of the hundreds of items are really dangerous. Therefore, your best line of defense is to suspect everything which is not a known and healthy food item.

Even a great number of plants, even those commonly found around the house, are poisonous. Teach your child never to eat any part of a plant unless it is served as food. This rule also applies to unknown berries and mushrooms. Even nibbling on leaves, sucking on plant stems is unsafe. Also, drinking water in which plants have been soaking can cause poisoning.

Some foods can be just as harmful as poisons when given to a child by mistake. For example, putting salt instead of sugar in baby's food can lead to illness. If you put sugar and salt into new jars, label them. Be sure to read the label each time before using.

If your child shows signs of poisoning, call your doctor right away.

Selection 45: Recalling Facts

1. Most child poisonings happen between the ages of
   ☐ a. one and three.   ☐ b. four and six.   ☐ c. eight and ten.

2. Poisonous products should be
   ☐ a. destroyed.   ☐ b. kept out of reach.   ☐ c. wrapped in newspaper.

3. Which of the following is a label warning?
   ☐ a. Contents under pressure
   ☐ b. For external use only
   ☐ c. Nonaerosal spray

4. A child can be poisoned by eating
   ☐ a. too much food.   ☐ b. raw vegetables.   ☐ c. unknown berries.

5. What should you do if your child shows signs of poisoning?
   ☐ a. Call your doctor   ☐ b. Call your neighbor   ☐ c. Wait 24 hours

Selection 45: Understanding Ideas

6. What is this article about?
   ☐ a. Drug abuse and poison
   ☐ b. Household poisoning
   ☐ c. Poison control centers

7. Children often get into poisons because they
   ☐ a. are curious.   ☐ b. are unsupervised.   ☐ c. want to help.

8. We can see that
   ☐ a. most children will not drink something that tastes bad.
   ☐ b. nearly all home products contain a harmful poison.
   ☐ c. mushrooms and berries are good for children to eat.

9. The writer makes this article clear by using
   ☐ a. facts.   ☐ b. opinions.   ☐ c. maps.

10 This article tells us that
   ☐ a doctors don't treat poison victims.
   ☐ b. house plants give off oxygen.
   ☐ c. too much salt can be harmful.

46. Satisfaction Guaranteed

It may take some time and effort to find the lawyer who will be right for you. It is wise to search for a family lawyer who can advise you about things before they happen. This way you can take your time. If you wait until you are in a jam, you may have to make a mad dash to find someone to represent you. You may not make the best choice if you are under pressure. Time spent selecting a lawyer is time well spent. The satisfaction you get from having made the right choice will make the search time all worth while.

One way to find a lawyer is to look for a satisfied client. Talk to your family and friends. See if they have used a lawyer whose services pleased them. Find out, too, what sort of matter the lawyer handled for them. Lawyers tend to specialize in a certain branch of the law. A lawyer may not want to handle a matter outside of his speciality.

Check to see if there is a lawyer referral service where you live. Such a service is often sponsored by the local bar association. If there is one, you will find it listed in the phone book. When you call, the service will give you the name of an attorney. Have a first interview with him for a stated fee. It should be a modest fee. At that meeting you can find out if you need further legal aid.

There may not be a referral service where you live. But there should be a local bar association. If so, you should find it listed in the phone book. Or you can ask at the county courthouse. Someone there will know the name of the president of the bar association and his address. You can then ask him for the name of a good lawyer. Make it clear that you are asking him as president of the bar association for his opinion. Tell him the kind of service you are seeking.

If you are poor and can't afford to pay a fee, you can get help. There may be a legal aid society where you live. Or there may be a group of lawyers who give free legal advice in certain cases. You can find out by looking in the phone book or by asking at the courthouse.

Selection 46: Recalling Facts

1. Finding the right lawyer takes
   - ☐ a. education and experience.
   - ☐ b. money and patience.
   - ☐ c. time and effort.

2. One good way to find a lawyer is to look for a
   - ☐ a. library.
   - ☐ b. police station.
   - ☐ c. satisfied client.

3. Lawyers tend to specialize in a certain branch of
   - ☐ a. law.
   - ☐ b. medicine.
   - ☐ c. politics.

4. A lawyer referral service is often sponsored by the local
   - ☐ a. aid association.
   - ☐ b. bar association.
   - ☐ c. court association.

5. Lawyer referral services may be listed in the
   - ☐ a. dictionary.
   - ☐ b. farmers almanac.
   - ☐ c. phone book.

Selection 46: Understanding Ideas

6. What would be a good title for this passage?
   - ☐ a. Famous Law Schools
   - ☐ b. How to Choose a Lawyer
   - ☐ c. History of Law

7. A good lawyer
   - ☐ a. gives free advice.
   - ☐ b. has few clients.
   - ☐ c. may be hard to find.

8. This passage hints that there are
   - ☐ a. few lawyers.
   - ☐ b. many branches of law.
   - ☐ c. not enough law schools.

9. Which of the following may give free legal advice?
   - ☐ a. The lawyer referral service
   - ☐ b. The legal aid society
   - ☐ c. The local bar association

10. We can see that
    - ☐ a. lawyers are only found in large cities.
    - ☐ b. poor people may get free legal advice.
    - ☐ c. the legal aid society charges a high fee.

47. A Good Experience

In one sense, an allowance is a child's share of the family income. It can be a good experience that parents can provide for their children. The amount should be what the family can afford. It should be given to the youngster to do with as she pleases. It should not be used as a tool to win the youngster's good behavior.

An allowance is not a bribe. It should be thought of as a learning tool. It can give a youngster first-hand experience in learning how to spend money. It can teach her how to get the best value for what she buys. It can help her use her skills in arithmetic.

Many youngsters make mistakes and buy unwisely at first. Some rush out to spend all their money the moment they get it. They forget that once it is spent, there will be no more for several days. From such haste, youngsters can learn how to choose wisely and spend carefully.

Parents need to know when to begin to give an allowance. They also want to decide how much to give. When a youngster starts school, she may want an allowance. She may have friends who receive one. A good time for considering an allowance may be when a youngster makes daily requests for ice cream or candy. This will help her to see the value of money.

At first a youngster may receive only half an allowance but get it twice a week. This would be a help to someone who finds a full week too long. A youngster will soon figure out that she can have two candy bars this week, or she can save her allowance for two weeks and buy a toy. She learns that she cannot have both the candy and the toy.

A wise parent will not control her child's buying. If a child makes her own mistakes with her own money, she is more apt to learn from her mistakes. Also, a child should not be made to save a part of each week's allowance. An allowance should not be taken away as punishment for bad behavior. An allowance should not be thought of as pay for doing household chores.

A youngster should be encouraged to be generous. An allowance should help her see that money isn't everything. No amount of money can buy friendship. Things such as love or respect do not have a price tag.

Selection 47: Recalling Facts

1. An allowance gives a child a chance to share in the family's
   - ☐ a. chores.
   - ☐ b. meals.
   - ☐ c. income.

2. The amount of an allowance should depend upon what the family can
   - ☐ a. afford.
   - ☐ b. borrow.
   - ☐ c. inherit.

3. An allowance can give a child the chance to use her
   - ☐ a. arithmetic skills.
   - ☐ b. map skills.
   - ☐ c. reading skills.

4. An allowance should be given once or twice
   - ☐ a. a week.
   - ☐ b. a month.
   - ☐ c. a year.

5. An allowance should not be used as a tool to win a child's
   - ☐ a. friends.
   - ☐ b. good behavior.
   - ☐ c. self-respect.

Selection 47: Understanding Ideas

6. Parents should give an allowance
   - ☐ a. to keep the child in line.
   - ☐ b. to pay a child for chores.
   - ☐ c. to teach the value of money.

7. We can see that children learn the value of money by
   - ☐ a. listening to friends.
   - ☐ b. making mistakes.
   - ☐ c. visiting the bank.

8. At first, most youngsters spend their money
   - ☐ a. foolishly.
   - ☐ b. carefully.
   - ☐ c. wisely.

9. An allowance should encourage a youngster to be
   - ☐ a. bold.
   - ☐ b. stingy.
   - ☐ c. unselfish.

10. This passage hints that giving the child an allowance
    - ☐ a. can be harmful to the child.
    - ☐ b. is a good experience for the child.
    - ☐ c. takes away the child's self-respect.

48. The Romantic Center

Reading Time _____

Comprehension Score _____

Words per Minute _____

Fireplaces tend to affect people in a strange way. They seem to have a romance all their own. Well they should. Fireplaces were once the center of family life. When the West was being settled, the fireplace was the only energy source in the home. It provided heat, light, and cooking facilities. We have all heard the tale of Abe Lincoln being born in a log cabin. He is said to have studied his law books in front of the open fire. He did his writing on the back of the fireplace shovel.

In large Colonial homes, there were a number of fireplaces. There would be one in the living room and another in the library. Often, there would be a fireplace in each bedroom. People burned logs in the open fireplace because logs were the only fuel that was around. Later, modern fireplaces burned "gas logs." These were artificial logs that were really gas outlets. Many of these are still around today.

As homes began to be built with heating furnaces, fireplaces started to disappear. While a few homes still had them, they were more for show than anything else. In fact, some of the fireplaces in today's homes are not really fireplaces at all. That is, they do not have hearths or chimneys or dampers or other things that a fireplace needs. It would be quite dangerous to build a real fire in one of these.

But today, fireplaces have begun to make a strong comeback. Part of this is due to the high cost of fuel and energy. People are using them more and more. With this new use, there is a need for people to learn the rules for fireplace safety.

There are some things we should all know about open fires in the home. For example, did you know that sparks can leap from an open fire? These sparks can ignite anything in the room that will burn. This is why a screen made of wire or special glass should be placed across the fireplace.

If charcoal is burned in a poorly vented fireplace, deadly gases could be released into the room. Logs you buy at the store are made of sawdust and wax. These should be handled differently from natural logs. They should be burned one at a time and not stacked.

A fireplace can be lovely. It can also be a killer if not used properly.

Selection 48: Recalling Facts

1. Fireplaces were once the center of
   □ a. early education.   □ b. family life.   □ c. social gatherings.

2. Later on in time, modern fireplaces burned
   □ a. dried leaves.   □ b. gas logs.   □ c. seasoned wood.

3. Today fireplaces have made a strong comeback because of the high cost of
   □ a. fuel.   □ b. groceries.   □ c. houses.

4. Charcoal can be a dangerous fuel because it
   □ a. does not burn.   □ b. shoots off sparks.   □ c. gives off deadly gases.

5. Logs you buy in the store are made of
   □ a. charcoal and wood.   □ b. newspaper and oil.   □ c. sawdust and wax.

Selection 48: Understanding Ideas

6. Fireplaces were
   □ a. important to the Colonists.
   □ b. invented by the English.
   □ c. never used in Europe.

7. It was usual for a large Colonial house
   □ a. to be built with one central fireplace.
   □ b. to have fireplaces for heating.
   □ c. to have a wood burning stove.

8. Some of the fireplaces in today's homes are used for
   □ a. cooking.   □ b. decoration.   □ c. storage.

9. Why is it good to use a fireplace screen?
   □ a. It adds decoration to the fireplace.
   □ b. It holds the logs in their proper place.
   □ c. It prevents sparks from leaving the fireplace.

10. If not used properly, a fireplace can be
    □ a. dangerous.
    □ b. sturdy.
    □ c. untidy.

49. Small but Mighty

Reading Time _____

Comprehension Score _____

Words per Minute _____

Wood decay is caused by small plants called fungi. These plants cannot live on wood that has a moisture content of less than about 30 percent. The wood in most well-built homes is safe because the moisture content is rarely about 15 percent. The way to stop decay is simple. Keep wood dry.

Keeping wood dry is not always that easy to do. The outside walls of a house are open to rain that blows against them. Soil carries water. It can wet any wood that touches it. Also, if there are plumbing leaks in your home, the inside wood can get wet.

Wood must be kept dry at all times because wood soaks up water and holds it for a long time. From time to time heavy rains can supply enough water for decay to begin.

If you know that wood will become wet, it can be protected. Wood can be treated with preservatives. For long term safety, the preservative should be put on under pressure. If the wood comes in touch with the ground, only pressure treatment will do the job. Some pieces of wood that only get wet from time to time can be treated to stop decay by brushing on a preservative. The correct chemical to use for treatment depends upon what the wood is used for. Some chemicals give off a terrible smell. These are not good for use indoors. Others cause paint to peel. You should mention what the wood is used for when you buy the preservative.

Mold and stain fungi can attack wood. Molds grow mainly on the surface but may get inside the outer sapwood. The dark color caused by mold on wood can be removed by light sanding. Stain fungi go beyond the outer layers and causes a dark color that cannot be removed. Both molds and stain feed on wood. By themselves, they do not decay or weaken the wood. But, they do increase the wood's ability to take on and hold moisture. Thus, they increase the possibility of future decay. If you see signs of mold and stain fungi, you may have a problem.

Wood decays slowly at temperatures below 40° F. So, decay is more rapid in the South than in the North. Decay is also more rapid in humid than in dry regions even though the plants which cause decay are present everywhere throughout the United States.

Selection 49: Recalling Facts

1. Wood decay is caused by small plants called
   - ☐ a. algae.
   - ☐ b. fungi.
   - ☐ c. germs.

2. In order to live, wood decaying plants need a moisture content of
   - ☐ a. 15 percent or less.
   - ☐ b. 25 percent.
   - ☐ c. 30 percent or more.

3. The wood in most well-built homes has a moisture content which is rarely above
   - ☐ a. 15 percent.
   - ☐ b. 30 percent.
   - ☐ c. 65 percent.

4. Which of the following is a good carrier of water?
   - ☐ a. Cloth
   - ☐ b. Iron
   - ☐ c. Soil

5. Wood can be protected from decay by using
   - ☐ a. cement.
   - ☐ b. preservatives.
   - ☐ c. water.

Selection 49: Understanding Ideas

6. Wood-decaying plants live well in wood that is
   - ☐ a. dry.
   - ☐ b. smooth.
   - ☐ c. wet.

7. The outside walls are constantly in contact with
   - ☐ a. insects.
   - ☐ b. moisture.
   - ☐ c. plants.

8. The best way to keep wood from decaying is to
   - ☐ a. keep it dry.
   - ☐ b. sand it.
   - ☐ c. split it.

9. Molds can cause wood to
   - ☐ a. bend and snap.
   - ☐ b. change color.
   - ☐ c. splinter easily.

10. The possibility of wood decay is high in the Southern United States because of the
    - ☐ a. higher temperatures.
    - ☐ b. many rivers.
    - ☐ c. salt water.

50. Better Safe Than Sorry

Reading Time _____

Comprehension Score _____

Words per Minute _____

Every year a great number of babies and young children die or are injured in fires. One out of every five fires is caused by careless smoking or by children playing with matches and lighters. Don't tempt children by leaving matches or lighters around a room.

Never leave a child alone in a house. In just a few seconds they could start a fire. Or a fire could start and trap them. A child will panic in a fire and will not know what to do. Unless a parent is around to help, a child may try to hide under a bed or in a closet. Home fire drills are a sound idea. The best way to stop panic in case of fire is to know what to do *before* a fire breaks out.

Your first thought in a fire should always be *escape.* Far too many people become victims because they do not know the killing power and speed of fire. If a fire is very small and has just started, you can put it out yourself. Do this if you have the proper tools on hand. In any case always send the children outside first. Smoke, not fire, is the real killer in a fire. According to studies, as many as eight out of ten deaths are due to inhaling fumes long before the flames ever came near the person.

Burns are another hazard to tots. Fireplaces, space heaters, floor furnaces and radiators have all caused horrible burns to babies. Since you cannot watch your child all the time, you must screen fireplaces. Put guards around heaters and radiators.

Some people use a vaporizer or portable heater in a child's room. If you do, be sure you place it out of reach. Be sure, too, that it is not placed too close to blankets or bedclothes.

Use care in the kitchen. It is not safe to let an infant crawl or a small child walk around the kitchen while you are preparing meals. There is danger of your tripping and spilling something hot on the child. There is even danger of a child pulling a hot pot off the stove on to herself. Also, do not use tablecloths that hang over the table edge. Children may grasp the cloth and pull hot foods down upon them. Be aware of these dangers and protect your child.

Selection 50: Recalling Facts

1. Careless smoking or children playing with matches and lighters cause
   - ☐ a. one out of five fires.
   - ☐ b. two out of three fires.
   - ☐ c. five out of ten fires.

2. Your first thought in a fire should always be
   - ☐ a. panic.
   - ☐ b. prevention.
   - ☐ c. escape.

3. What is the real killer in a fire?
   - ☐ a. The flames
   - ☐ b. The fuel
   - ☐ c. The smoke

4. How many people die each year from inhaling deadly smoke fumes?
   - ☐ a. Two out of three
   - ☐ b. Five out of eight
   - ☐ c. Eight out of ten

5. Burns can be caused by
   - ☐ a. harmful toys.
   - ☐ b. old tin cans.
   - ☐ c. space heaters.

Selection 50: Understanding Ideas

6. We can see that
   - ☐ a. adults know how to handle fires.
   - ☐ b. many children start fires in the home.
   - ☐ c. some firemen are not well trained.

7. When children are trapped in a fire, they often become
   - ☐ a. confused.
   - ☐ b. happy.
   - ☐ c. silly.

8. The best way to stop panic in the case of fire is
   - ☐ a. to be prepared.
   - ☐ b. to call a neighbor.
   - ☐ c. to run away.

9. Using vaporizers in a child's room can be
   - ☐ a. dangerous.
   - ☐ b. funny.
   - ☐ c. untidy.

10. Many fires start because
    - ☐ a. fire departments are rare.
    - ☐ b. people don't respect fire.
    - ☐ c. someone was careless.

Answer Key

Progress Graph

Pacing Graph

Answer Key

	1.	2.	3.	4.	5.	6.	7.	8.	9.	10.
1.	1. c	2. a	3. c	4. b	5. b	6. b	7. b	8. c	9. c	10. b
2.	1. a	2. b	3. c	4. a	5. b	6. b	7. a	8. b	9. b	10. c
3.	1. c	2. b	3. b	4. a	5. b	6. a	7. c	8. b	9. c	10. a
4.	1. b	2. a	3. b	4. a	5. a	6. c	7. b	8. b	9. b	10. c
5.	1. a	2. b	3. c	4. a	5. c	6. c	7. b	8. c	9. b	10. a
6.	1. c	2. c	3. c	4. c	5. c	6. c	7. b	8. a	9. a	10. c
7.	1. a	2. c	3. b	4. c	5. a	6. c	7. b	8. b	9. a	10. a
8.	1. b	2. b	3. a	4. b	5. b	6. b	7. b	8. c	9. a	10. a
9.	1. b	2. a	3. a	4. c	5. b	6. c	7. a	8. c	9. a	10. b
10.	1. a	2. c	3. b	4. a	5. b	6. c	7. c	8. b	9. b	10. c
11.	1. c	2. a	3. c	4. c	5. c	6. a	7. c	8. a	9. a	10. b
12.	1. b	2. c	3. c	4. b	5. a	6. a	7. c	8. b	9. c	10. c
13.	1. a	2. b	3. a	4. b	5. c	6. a	7. c	8. c	9. a	10. b
14.	1. a	2. a	3. c	4. b	5. c	6. b	7. b	8. a	9. a	10. c
15.	1. c	2. a	3. c	4. b	5. c	6. a	7. b	8. b	9. c	10. a
16.	1. c	2. b	3. c	4. b	5. c	6. b	7. b	8. c	9. a	10. a
17.	1. b	2. a	3. c	4. c	5. a	6. a	7. a	8. a	9. b	10. b
18.	1. a	2. a	3. c	4. a	5. a	6. b	7. b	8. a	9. c	10. a
19.	1. c	2. b	3. c	4. c	5. c	6. b	7. c	8. b	9. c	10. a
20.	1. b	2. c	3. b	4. b	5. a	6. a	7. a	8. b	9. a	10. c
21.	1. a	2. a	3. b	4. a	5. c	6. a	7. a	8. a	9. b	10. b
22.	1. a	2. c	3. a	4. a	5. b	6. a	7. b	8. b	9. a	10. c
23.	1. a	2. c	3. b	4. c	5. a	6. b	7. a	8. c	9. a	10. a
24.	1. c	2. c	3. b	4. c	5. c	6. a	7. a	8. b	9. a	10. a
25.	1. a	2. c	3. b	4. a	5. b	6. b	7. c	8. b	9. a	10. a

Answer Key

26.	1. c	2. a	3. a	4. c	5. c	6. b	7. b	8. a	9. b	10. c
27.	1. a	2. c	3. a	4. a	5. c	6. b	7. b	8. b	9. b	10. b
28.	1. b	2. a	3. c	4. c	5. a	6. b	7. c	8. b	9. c	10. b
29.	1. a	2. a	3. a	4. b	5. b	6. b	7. b	8. c	9. a	10. a
30.	1. b	2. a	3. c	4. c	5. a	6. a	7. c	8. a	9. c	10. b
31.	1. b	2. c	3. b	4. a	5. b	6. b	7. b	8. a	9. b	10. b
32.	1. a	2. b	3. a	4. c	5. c	6. c	7. b	8. b	9. b	10. c
33	1. a	2. b	3. b	4. b	5. a	6. b	7. b	8. c	9. a	10. b
34.	1. b	2. c	3. c	4. b	5. c	6. b	7. b	8. a	9. b	10. a
35.	1. b	2. c	3. c	4. a	5. c	6. b	7. a	8. a	9. a	10. b
36.	1. b	2. a	3. c	4. b	5. b	6. b	7. b	8. a	9. b	10. b
37.	1. b	2. c	3. c	4. b	5. b	6. c	7. b	8. a	9. b	10. a
38.	1. b	2. a	3. a	4. a	5. c	6. a	7. a	8. a	9. a	10. a
39.	1. c	2. a	3. c	4. c	5. b	6. b	7. b	8. c	9. c	10. b
40.	1. c	2. b	3. a	4. a	5. c	6. a	7. b	8. a	9. a	10. a
41.	1. a	2. c	3. a	4. c	5. a	6. b	7. a	8. a	9. a	10. a
42.	1. b	2. a	3. a	4. a	5. b	6. b	7. c	8. b	9. b	10. b
43.	1. a	2. c	3. b	4. b	5. c	6. a	7. c	8. c	9. c	10. b
44.	1. c	2. b	3. b	4. b	5. a	6. b	7. b	8. c	9. a	10. c
45.	1. a	2. b	3. b	4. c	5. a	6. b	7. a	8. b	9. a	10. c
46.	1. c	2. c	3. a	4. b	5. c	6. b	7. c	8. b	9. b	10. b
47.	1. c	2. a	3. a	4. a	5. b	6. c	7. b	8. a	9. c	10. b
48.	1. b	2. b	3. a	4. c	5. c	6. a	7. b	8. b	9. c	10. a
49.	1. b	2. c	3. a	4. c	5. b	6. c	7. b	8. a	9. b	10. a
50.	1. a	2. c	3. c	4. c	5. c	6. b	7. a	8. a	9. a	10. c

Progress Graph (1-25)

Directions: Write your comprehension score in the box under the selection number. Then put an *x* on the line under each box to show your reading time and words-per-minute reading rate.

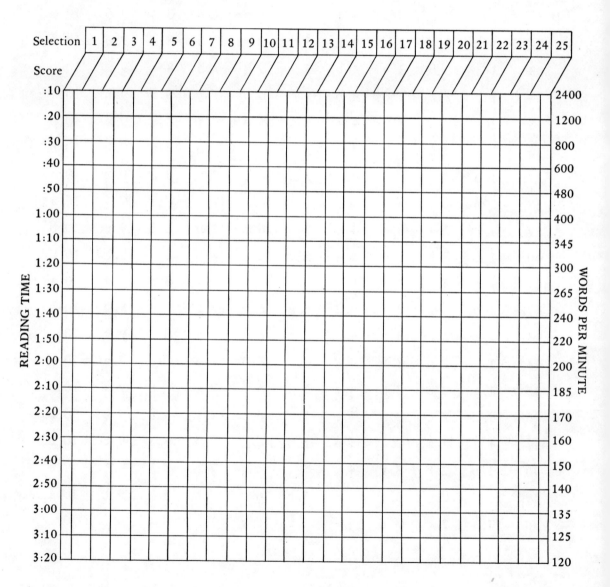

Progress Graph (26-50)

Directions: Write your comprehension score in the box under the selection number. Then put an *x* on the line under each box to show your reading time and words-per-minute reading rate.

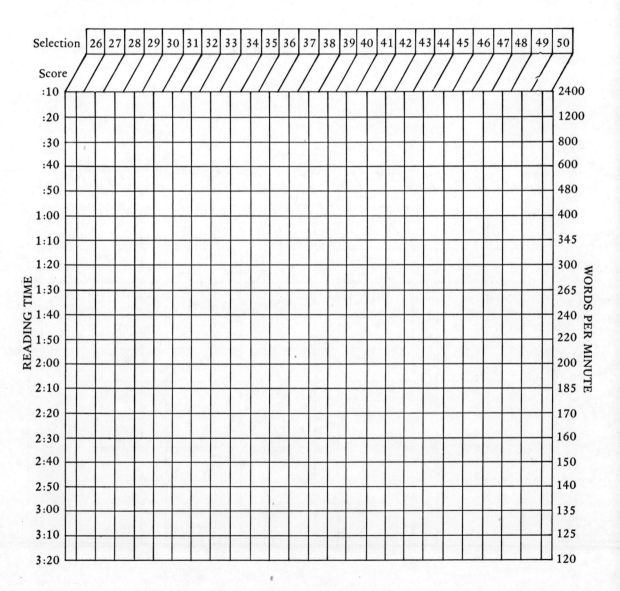

Selection	26 27 28 29 30 31 32 33 34 35 36 37 38 39 40 41 42 43 44 45 46 47 48 49 50	

Score	READING TIME	WORDS PER MINUTE
:10		2400
:20		1200
:30		800
:40		600
:50		480
1:00		400
1:10		345
1:20		300
1:30		265
1:40		240
1:50		220
2:00		200
2:10		185
2:20		170
2:30		160
2:40		150
2:50		140
3:00		135
3:10		125
3:20		120

Pacing Graph

Directions: In the boxes labeled "Pace" along the top of the graph, write in your words-per-minute rate. On the vertical line under each box, put an *x* to indicate your comprehension score.

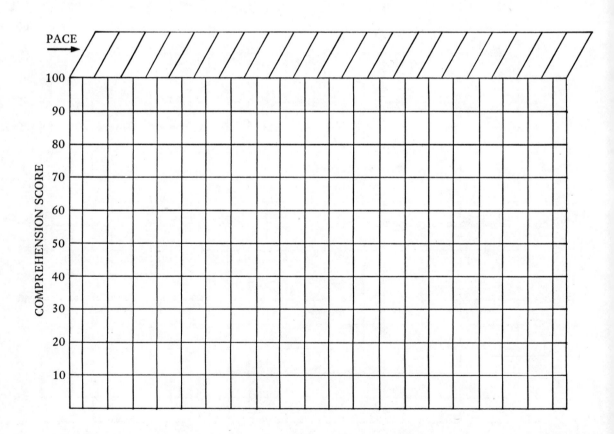